Li GREECE

Lyn Waldie

PRO LINGUA ◯ **ASSOCIATES**

Pro Lingua Associates, Publishers

P.O. Box 1348
Brattleboro, Vermont 05302, USA

Webstore: www.ProLinguaAssociates.com
Office:802-257-7779
Orders: 800-366-4775
Email: Orders@ProLinguaAssociates.com
Info@ProLinguaAssociates.com
SAN 216-0579

Published in Celebration of
The 2004 Summer Olympic Games
in Athens, Greece

This book follows the general format of the *Living In* series originally developed by The Experiment in International Living, now known as World Learning, in Brattleboro, Vermont, as part of its Orientation Development Project. Peter deJong, former Secreatry General, and the directors of the various Experiment in International Living National Offices identified the original content areas covered in this country-specific series. The initial development funds were provided by the U. S. Information Agency under the President's International Youth Initiative. Pro Lingua is grateful for permission to continue the publication of the series.

This book was designed and set by A. A. Burrows in a text type face called Palatino. Although modern, it is based on Renaissance designs typical of the Palatinate area in Germany. Palatino is an elegant face, the most widely used, and pirated, face of the twentieth century. It was designed by Hermann Zapf in 1948 in Frankfurt. For contrast, the chapter titles are set in a caligraphic Adobe type face called Bible Script. The book was printed and bound by Boyd Printing in Albany, New York.

First edition, first printing 2004. 1000 copies in print.
Printed in the United States of America.

Contents

Introduction   1

First Steps   2
  Money   2
  Food   4
  Drinks   7
  Dining Out   8
  Hotels   9
  Telephone and Internet   10
  The Post Office   10
  Media   10
  Transportation   11
  Shopping   13
  Markets   15
  Kiosks   16
  Health and Medical Care   16
  Pharmacies   16
  Clothing   17
  Security   18
  Strikes   18
  Tipping   18
  Conversions   18
  Electricity   20
  Pets   20
  Leisure Activities   21
  Cultural Life   21
  Museums and Archeological
    Sites   22
  Night Life   22
  Sports   23
  Finding a Place to Live   24
  Paying Bills   24
  Residence Visas and Work
    Permits   24
  Picking Up Work   26

Customs and Values   27
  Caveat   27
  The Village   27
  Cafeníos   28
  Family Life   28
  Religion   29

What's in a Name   31
Name Day Celebrations   32
Rites of Passage   33
Festivals   35
National Holidays   38

Cross-Cultural Issues   39
  Contradictions in
    Character   39
  Greetings   39
  Conversation   40
  Communication Style   40
  Gestures   41
  Time   42
  Personal Space   42
  Courtesy   43
  Privacy   43
  The Bureaucracy   43
  Connections   44
  Rules and Regulations   44
  The Evil Eye   44
  Hospitality   45
  Smoking   45
  Greek Cultural Terms   45

Country Facts   48
  History   48
    *A Brief Outline of Greek
      History*   49
    Neolithic Period   49
    Minoan Period   49
    Mycenaean Period   51
    "Dark Ages"   53
    Archaic Period   53
    The Twelve Olympians   55
    Classical Period   56
    Hellenistic Period   57
    Roman Period   58
    Byzantine Period   59
    Ottoman Period   61
    War of Independence   61
    Modern Greek Period   62

CONTENTS

The Land   64
The People   65
The New Immigrants   65
A Map of Greece   66
Government   68
Economy   68
Education   69
Literature   69
Theater   70
Folk Art   71
Music   72
Dances   74

The Greek Language   75
Pronunciation Guide   76
Some Basic Grammar   78
  Definite Articles   78
  Nouns and Adjectives   78
  Personal Pronouns   78
  Possessive Adjectives   82
  Verbs   79
  Question Words   82
  Can and Must   82
  Some Useful Conjunctions
    and Adverbs   83

Prepositions   83
Numbers   83
Time Words   84
Other Useful Words   84
Some Useful Expressions
  and Vocabulary   85
Getting Around   85
Some Typical Greek
  Expressions   86

Resources   88
Some Useful Websites
  ... and Phone Numbers   88
Some Books about Greece   89
  Ancient History   89
  Modern Greek History   89
  Ethnology   90
  Religion   90
Greek Literature
  In Translation   90
Stories about Greece   91
Travel Writing   91
A Cookbook   92
Movies in English
  about Greece   92

Also Available
from Pro Lingua Associates

Living in France
Living in Italy
Living in Japan
Living in Mexico
Living in Spain
Living in South Korea
Living in the United States

iv

Living in Greece

Introduction

Note on the transliteration of Greek words used in the English text: delta (δ) is dh, theta (ϑ) is th, chi (χ) is ch, all long e (η, ι, υ, ει, οι) are i, gamma (γ) is y or g, short e (ε) is e.

You'll have a great adventure living or traveling in Greece. Greece is not only home to one of the world's oldest civilizations; it is also a modern seaside paradise with white-washed Aegean islands bathed in sunshine. There's an island to appeal to everyone's taste ranging from trendy and lively to isolated and quiet. Athens is a living museum steeped in history, and a bustling metropolis that never sleeps. It's also one of the safest places in Europe to travel in. English is widely spoken making it quite easy to get around. There are also some challenges to living in Greece. Dealing with bureaucracy in one form or another is typically the main problem. And the chaotic traffic and smog in Athens can also get on your nerves.

This guide is an introduction to Greece. It'll help you plan your trip, and get you oriented once you're there. **First Steps** covers such topics as money, food, finding a place to stay, and shopping - the practical things you need to know when going to a new country. There's also information on finding work and getting visas if you plan to stay there for any length of time. **Customs and Values** looks at some of the Greek traditions such as marriage and baptism, name days, and the importance of family and religion. **Cross-cultural Issues** takes a look at communication styles, as well as attitudes towards time and space to help you make sense of your new environment. There's also an overview of cultural points like the evil eye, and some Greek words describing uniquely Greek cultural aspects. **Country Facts** has an overview of Greek history and a rough guide to the arts such as poetry, music, dance, and folk art traditions. In **Greek Language** you'll find a mini-grammar, some vocabulary, and some useful expressions to get you started. **Books About Greece** is a selected bibliography of books written about Greece.

First Steps

Money

Exchange. The Euro is the currency in Greece, as in most of the European Union. The exchange rate to the dollar is approximately 1:1, but it fluctuates according to world market conditions. The Euro (€) comes in the following denominations: The bank notes are €5, €10, €20, €50, €100, €200, €500; the coins are 1 cent, 2 cent, 5 cent, 10 cent, 20 cent, 50 cent, €1, and €2. This money is used in Greece and in Austria, Belgium, Finland, France, Germany, Ireland, Italy, Luxembourg, the Netherlands, Portugal, and Spain. This means that it is now possible to travel from Greece around most of Europe without exchanging money. Great Britain and the Scandinavian countries are considering adopting the Euro as well.

About the Euro bank notes. Unlike the U.S. dollar, the Euro notes come in different sizes and colors. They range in size from the €5 at 120 x 62 mm to the €500 at 160 x 82 mm. The colors are €5 grey, €10 red, €20 blue, €50 orange, €100 green, €200 yellow-brown, €500 purple. Each bill has an architectural element using an arch on one side and a collage of a map of Europe and a bridge on the other. The beautiful buildings shown are not real buildings but ideal examples of European architecture, each typical of a different style and historical period; the advantage of using virtual architecture is that using actual Italian buildings would have angered the French, etc. The periods are €5 Classic, €10 Romanesque, €20 Gothic, €50 Renaissance, €100 Baroque/Rococo, €200 19th Century Iron and Glass Structures, and €500 20th Century Modern.

About the Euro coins. Like the notes, the Euro coins are varied and interesting. The largest is the €2. This is a brass or "gold" colored coin with a "silver" colored ring around it. The €1 coin is the reverse, silver with a gold ring. The other coins are brass colored. The €2 is larger than the €1, and they have distinctive edges. The 50 cent coin is slightly larger than the €1, but has a different edge and is thinner. The 20, 10, 5, 2, and 1 cent coins get progressively smaller, and each coin has a distinctive edge. Additional complication and interest comes from the decoration on the coins. One side is standard, but the other side has a national design. For example, all the Dutch coins show the head of the queen of the Netherlands.

The Greek coins are particularly interesting since each has a different image. The 2 Euro coin shows a scene from a mosaic of Sparta in the 3rd Century, A.D., showing the abduction of Europa by Zeus, as a bull. The 1 Euro coin is modeled after a 5th Century, B.C., Athenian 4 drachma coin depicting the owl of Athena. On the 10, 20, and 50 cent coins are the heads of leaders of the Greek independence struggle: on the 50¢, Eleftherios Venizelos (1864-1936); on the 20¢, Ioannis Capodistrias (1776-1831); and on the 10¢, Rigas-Fereos (1757-98). And on the 1, 2, and 5 cent coins the Greeks have put ships as symbols of the vital role shipping has always played in their lives. The 5¢ shows a modern tanker, the 2¢ a corvette from the time of the War of Independence (1821-27), and the 1¢ a large Athenian trireme, a warship from the "Golden Age" of Athenian democracy, the 5th Century, B.C. No matter where the Euro coins come from, they can be used in any country using the Euro.

The most convenient way to obtain money is by ATM. These are located throughout the country and accept common banking systems such as Visa, MasterCard, and Cirrus. Traveler's checks can be exchanged at banks and tourist offices; the rate may vary slightly from place to place and some may charge a small fee. You can also take cash advances on credit cards at certain banks. Most large hotels, restaurants, and shops accept credit cards. Don't be surprised if you are offered a "discount" to pay in cash instead at some shops. At smaller places like *tavernas*, pensions, and small shops you might want to check first whether or not credit cards are accepted. Banks are open from about 8 a.m. to 2 p.m., Monday through Friday. Accounts can be opened in euros, other European currencies, or dollars at most banks. Checks are rarely, if ever, used in Greece. Most personal transactions, including paying bills, are paid in cash in person.

Food

Greek food is well known internationally, but there are some specialties that are rarely enjoyed outside of Greece. There's nothing like sitting at a *taverna* by the sea and eating freshly caught grilled octopus with a delicious Greek salad, or sitting in a farmer's kitchen and experiencing the legendary Greek hospitality with some homemade feta, olives, bread, and wine from the barrel.

Appetizers (mezédhes) are eaten at any time of day. Some typical ones are:

tzatzíki - yogurt, cucumber, and garlic dip
taramasaláta – red caviar dip
melantzánasalata - eggplant dip
yigantés - broad beans in tomato sauce
dolmádhes - stuffed grape leaves
avgolémono soúpa - egg lemon soup.

These are always served with bread (*psomí*) and a drink.

Bread (psomí) is a staple and served with every meal. You can buy it at most supermarkets or fresh from the *foúrnos* (oven/bakery). If you get there early enough, the bread will be hot from the oven. Bread is purchased by the kilo or half kilo (*misó kiló*). The most common kinds are white (*áspro*) or dark (*mávro*), but you can also find eight grain (*octósporo*) and other varieties. In *tavernas* and restaurants, bread is served sliced in a basket for a small extra charge, which will be the "cover" charge on your bill. Butter is not generally served with bread except at breakfast or at fine restaurants.

Fish (psári) and seafood in general are loved and honored in Greece. When the fishermen return, passersby stop to admire the catch or buy some directly from them. There is a wide variety of seafood ranging from lobster to smelt. A *taverna* by the sea is the best place to get fresh fish and has to be one of the quintessential experiences of being in Greece. Oftentimes the taverna owner is a fisherman himself who will have been fishing during the night. Some restaurants in towns have fresh fish, but you should ask to see the fish first, determine its freshness, and then choose the one you want. Fish soup, *kakaviá*, is a delicious specialty not to be missed.

4

 Some typical Greek fish are: red mullet (*barboúni*), sea bass (*pláki*), swordfish (*xifías*), red snapper (*sinagrídha*), and sea bream (*fangrí*). In a restaurant these fish are priced by the kilo and can be quite expensive. Less expensive and priced by the plate are grilled octopus (*chtapódhi*), fried squid (*kalamári*), batter fried salted cod (*bakaliáros*) served with garlic sauce (*skordaliá*), and a smelt-like small fish (*marídhes*) which is lightly fried and eaten head and all.

Gathered Food. Certain seafood like sea urchins (*achinós*) and periwinkles (*patalídhes*) is sometimes gathered and eaten raw, on the spot, with a bit of lemon and bread to scoop up the roe or flesh. If you catch your own fish, some *tavernas* will prepare it for you for a small fee. Mushrooms (*manitária*) and snails (*tsalingária*) are gathered after the first rains in the fall. The mushrooms are usually sautéed. The snails are cleaned, a process that takes several days, and then cooked in a sauce. You will find wild greens (*chórta*) in nearly every *taverna*. Since there are different varieties, these greens are available year round. They are boiled and served with lemon and oil. Capers (*káperi*) grow in the rocks on hillsides in many parts of Greece. The buds of the caper flower are collected in the spring and, like olives, they need marinating before eating. Sage, chamomile, and other herbs for tea grow on the hillsides. Special to the Mediterranean is Greek Mountain tea, which cures all kinds of illnesses. Thyme, oregano, and rosemary also grow wild and are frequently gathered for use at home. Basil plants bring good luck and are grown in pots at home. Rabbit and birds are hunted in the autumn and can sometimes be ordered in *tavernas*.

Meat. Lamb (*arní*), the traditional meat of Greece, is prepared a number of ways – roasted with a delicious egg lemon sauce, or charcoal roasted on a spit. Grilled lamb chops (*paidhákia*), smaller and tastier than the American variety, are seasoned with oregano and lemon; there is no mint sauce here! Wild rabbit stew(*stifádho*) seasoned with garlic, onions and bay, is available in season. *Souvláki* (skewered meat, shish kebab) is usually pork but may also be lamb, beef, or chicken. *Kléftiko* is meat, potatoes, and vegetable cooked together in foil. During the Ottoman occupation, the Turks called the rebels who fought in the Greek resistance bandits or *Kléfts* (as in "clepto," to steal). *Kléftiko*, neatly wrapped up, was carried by their relatives to the bandits in hiding.

5

Dairy Products. Yogurt (*yaoúrti*) is delicious in Greece. The secret is that it is strained and not at all runny. Although the traditional kind has 10% fat, there are also 5%, 2% and 0% varieties available that keep their flavor and texture. Yaoúrti is delicious with Greek honey (*méli*) and fresh fruit. It's also a good substitute for sour cream, which is rarely available in Greece. Most familiar European cheeses are available in the supermarket.

Greek cheeses (*tiri*). There are many delicious kinds. These include:

Féta - salty moist goat's cheese, served in Greek salads
Kasséri - firm and mild like Provolone, served sliced or in fried cheese (*saganáki*)
Kafalotirí - hard, aged, strong flavored cheese, like Romano
Graviéra - creamy and rich like Gruyere, served as an appetizer or dessert. There are special *graviéra* cheeses from all over Greece, each with its own distinctive taste.
Mezíthra - soft, mild cheese served fresh, available in the spring.
Káftotiri - a spicy creamy cheese.

Some regions specialize in certain cheeses, so be sure to ask around.

Other Greek specialties include: olives (*eliés*), olive oil (*elioládhon* or *ládhi*), honey (*méli*), wine (*krasí*), dried figs (*síka*), and pistachios (*fastíkia*). All familiar fresh fruit and vegetables are available in Greece in season. The famous Greek Salad with tomatoes, cucumber, onion, green pepper, feta, and doused with olive oil is called *choriátiki* (village salad).

For special food served on holidays see *Festivals* on page35.

Drinks

Coffee. Greek coffee, *ellenikó kafé*, is served in a demitasse cup with the coffee grounds on the bottom. It's prepared one cup at a time in a small, long-handled brass pot called a *bríki*. The powdered coffee, sugar, and water are boiled until it foams. The more foam, *kaimáki*, the better the coffee. It always comes with a glass of water, and it can be ordered sweet (*glikó*), semi-sweet (*métrio*), or without sugar (*skétos*). (Older women in the villages read the dregs of the coffee to predict the future.) Greeks are rightly proud of their invention called the *frappé*, a cold coffee made with Nescafe and very popular all over the country. Espresso, Cappuccino, Fredo, and French coffee (drip) are also available in Greece.

Wines vary from region to region. *Retsina* is probably the best known wine, but it seems to be losing its popularity, especially with young people. Although some people feel it has a slight turpentine taste, it grows on you once you get used to it. *Retsina* goes well with Greek food, which tends to be oily. Greece also produces many types of excellent red, white, and rose wines. Bottled wines are available in markets and in restaurants. *Boutari* or *Cambas* are good medium-priced wines. You can't go wrong with a red wine from *Nemea* (Peloponnese) or *Naoussa* (Macedonia). Good white wines come from Santorini, Cephallonia, and other islands. Crete has several good red and white wines. Local wine, no matter where you are in Greece, is best when served from the barrel or "open" (*chíma krasí*). You can buy it directly from some farmers or vintners if you bring your own five-kilo jug (*gallóni*) or a plastic water bottle. Note that wine is weighed in Greece, and sold by the kilo, not by the liter.

Beer (*bíra*) is available in many of the common European varieties. Many of the brands are bottled in Greece. *Mythos* is a good Greek beer, *Kaiser*, if you prefer malt, and even *Bud* (American) is available. The beer labeled *Budweiser* in Europe is the original from the Czech Republic.

Spirits. The best-known Greek spirit is *ouzo*, an anise flavored aperitif. It's usually mixed with water, which turns it a milky white. Related to *ouzo* are regional varieties of *tsíporo* (or *tsikoudhiá* in Crete), which comes with or without the anise flavor. These drinks should be served with an appetizer or mezé (*mezedháki*). The most famous Greek brandy, Konyák, is *Metaxas*, available in 3 grades: 3, 5 and 7 star.

Dining Out

Greeks generally eat dinner around 10 p.m., or even later in the summer. Menus are posted outside the door. Restaurants are categorized by the government, and prices are set accordingly. If you're up for a splurge, you can pick out a restaurant by the linen tablecloths and wine glasses. If you're on a budget, look for a cozy *taverna*. Fruit is usually served after dinner, and sometimes it is *gratis* from the restaurant owner. Dessert isn't common in Greece, and you probably won't find dessert or coffee in most *tavernas*, although restaurants may serve them. (see *Cafes* and *Cafeníos*).

Tavernas are the traditional Greek dining experience. The food is prepared in the morning, although grilled items are cooked to order. Sometimes there's meat roasting on a spit outside. In some of the older tavernas it's common practice for customers to go into the kitchen to see what looks most appealing. Most tavernas offer wine from the barrel (*chíma krasí*) by the kilo, half kilo, or quarter kilo. Most dining is outdoors, either overlooking the sea, in a cozy garden, or at tables spilling out into the street.

Restaurants (*estiatória*) tend to be more expensive than *tavernas*. They often serve international, as well as Greek cuisine. They usually serve bottled wines and some of the more exclusive restaurants might have foreign wines. There are also ethnic restaurants, like Mexican, Chinese, or Indian, springing up in Athens and some tourist spots. Sushi seems to have caught on as well.

Mezádhiko, Ouzádhiko, Tsiporádhiko all serve various appetizers (*mézes*) meant to be shared by the table and served with *ouzo* or *tsíporo*. These *ádhikos* make for a very convivial evening out with your friends.

Fast Food, take out, and self-service are ubiquitous in cities and tourist areas. A traditional Greek "fast food" is *yéros* (called *gyros* in the U.S.), pressed pork sliced off a large skewer and served in pita bread with tomatoes, onions and *tzadziki*. *Souvláki* is the same only with small bits of skewered meat. Other fast foods are: cheese pie (*tirópita*), spinach pie (*spanikópita*), and custard pie (*bougátsa*). There are also plenty of western style fast food such as pizza, hamburgers, and French fries (*tzíps*).

Cafés serve coffee and sweets. You can stay all day in a *café* drinking one cup of coffee and not be rushed away. All types of coffee (see *Coffee* on page 7) are usually available. *Café* life is important in Greece. "Let's go for a coffee" (*Páme yia café*) is an often-heard expression. *Cafés* are everywhere and they are often crowded. There are even Starbucks in several locations around Athens.

Cafeníos are traditionally men's coffee houses. Mostly older men go to them today to meet with their friends, discuss politics, drink coffee, and play cards or backgammon (*távli*).

Zacharoplastíons (Sweet shops) serve famous Greek sweets like *baklava* and *kataifi*. This is the place to get pastry, candy, or liquor to take to someone's house when you are a guest. You can also get a cold drink or snack here. Ice cream is available in season.

Hotels

Hotels are categorized and priced by the Greek government as deluxe, A, B, or C. There are also pensions or "rooms to let" which are also categorized as A, B, or C. Sometimes the "rooms to let" are in peoples' homes and are spotlessly clean. If you're free spirited and traveling on a budget, you can generally find a reasonably priced room by taking one from one of the pension owners who meet the ferryboats. Although, in mid-season rooms are at a premium. You should agree on the price and find out the location and amenities (like private toilet) before you go to the pension. If you feel more secure having a reservation somewhere, or want more comfortable accommodation, you should book in advance through a travel agent or call the hotel yourself. Government regulations require that all room prices be displayed in the rooms.

The tourist season is from April through October. The high peak season is July and August when hotel reservations are essential. The best times to travel are spring and fall when the weather's still good and there are fewer tourists. November through March is considered off-season when you can bargain for a room; however, many places close in the winter.

Telephone and Internet

The easiest way to use a public phone is to buy a telephone card from kiosks (*períptera*) or other convenient locations. You can also make a call from kiosks or hotels. However, there's a small surcharge on the metered phones at kiosks, and hotels may charge as much as a 50% surcharge. You can also make credit card calls using AT&T, Sprint, or MCI; dial the access number for the respective company.

Cell phones (*kinitá*) are widely used in Greece, as you will discover the minute you arrive. There is no charge for an incoming call, but the rate to call a cell phone from another cell phone or a land line is higher than the normal land line rate. The rate is the same all over the country, even if you're calling a cell phone in the same city. Greece operates on the GSM network. Cosmote, Telestet, and Vodafone offer roaming facilities.

There are many local Internet access companies in Greece, and it is quite easy to set up Internet access from your home through one of them. There is also Internet access in some hotels if you have your own laptop. Internet cafes are also plentiful all over the country.

The Post Office

The post office (*tachidromío*) opens at 7:30 a.m., Monday through Friday, and closes anytime between 1:30 and 8 p.m., depending on the area. Some post offices are open on Saturday as well. You can have your mail sent to *poste restante* (general delivery) and pick it up at the post office. *Poste restante* mail will generally be held for at least a month before being returned. If you receive a large package from outside the EU, you will receive a notification to pick it up at the post office and may need to pay a customs fee depending on the value.

Media

An English language newspaper, the weekly *Athens News,* comes out on Friday. In addition to news from Greece, there are ferry schedules and weekend pharmacy hours, as well as movie and TV listings. There's also the daily *Herald Tribune,* published in Greece, with a Greek supplement from *Kathimerini* newspaper. *Odyssey* is an excellent bi-monthly glossy magazine, covering issues related to Greece and Greeks abroad.

These are all available at kiosks in most towns throughout the country. You'll also be able to find American and British magazines and newspapers, but they're sometimes twice as expensive as what you pay at home. There are many American TV programs aired in Greece in English with Greek subtitles.

You may want to invest in a short-wave radio to pick up the BBC or VOA in order to get news coverage in English in Greece. Throughout Greece, National Public Radio's 24-hour service is available on both the Hotbird Satellite and the WorldSpace portable digital radio system and as part of American Forces Network at 107.0 FM. You can also listen to NPR stations and many others streamed on line over the internet. In some areas you can get CNN and CBS News on TV. Greeks are avid newspaper readers and are well informed on the political events within Greece. Greek newspapers are aligned to specific political parties.

Transportation

Airplanes. There are two domestic airlines, Olympic Airways and Aegean which have regular flights to all accessible destinations within Greece as well as internationally. Domestic flights cost about four times more than buses or ferries. There is a brand new airport in Athens, which runs quite efficiently (unless there is a strike).

Transport to the airport. To get from the airport, there is a frequent and convenient bus/metro route (Buses E94 or E95) or you can take a taxi. The airport buses run all night. Buses also run from the airport to Piraeus (E96). Allow about an hour to get from the airport to the city center.

Ferryboats. Most ferries leave from the port of Piraeus, which you can easily reach by metro or taxi. You can travel either economy or first class. If you're making an over-night journey, different ferry lines offer varying types of sleeping accommodations, from a basic 6-person dorm to luxurious suites. All of these boats have a snack bar and restaurant (with meals offered at various times), and some even have a swimming pool. Cars and motorcycles can be taken on the ferries. Boat schedules are listed in newspapers, or posted in tourist offices. In season, ferry tickets should definitely be purchased in advance through a travel agent or over the Internet (only on certain lines). Be aware that not all travel agents sell tickets for all ferry lines and may not even know about the lines for which they don't sell tickets. You can also buy tickets at the departure gate from a kiosk. Ferry service is regular and reliable. For up-to-date ferry schedules you can check out www.gtp.gr or call the tourist police on 171.

Hydrofoils (sometimes called Flying Dolphins) are twice as fast as the ferries and about twice as expensive. Tickets should be purchased in advance for a reserved seat. Hydrofoils run year round to the Saronic Islands, and in season to the Cyclades, Crete, and other islands. There is both economy and first class, and some of the bigger ones can take cars.

Buses. Buses are the usual way of getting around on mainland Greece (KTEL). There are two bus stations in Athens, one for northern Greece and another for the Peloponnese. You need to reserve a seat for the long routes, which can be made on the spot. If, however, a bus is already booked and they don't add another one for that time slot you may need to wait for the next one. Buses tend to be fairly frequent. On long routes there is a rest stop to break up the journey.

On short routes, such as on the islands or from village to village, fares are collected on the bus by a ticket taker, and you don't need to have the exact fare. In the less touristy areas the schedule may be a little erratic. Buses are generally punctual in their departure time, sometimes even leaving a minute or two early.

Trains. There are both slow trains with many stops and express trains (intercity). The intercity trains are probably the most comfortable way of traveling on mainland Greece, but they only go to a few locations and not as frequently as the buses travel. There are both first and second classes on trains. Tickets for Intercity Rail can be purchased in advance over the phone and delivered to your home for a small fee, or at the central ticket and information office at 6 Sina Street. Eurail Passes can also be used.

Taxis. Taxis are inexpensive in Athens compared to the rest of Europe. Getting a taxi in Athens can be difficult during rush hour, and drivers will nearly always collect other passengers on the way. The way to hail a cab is to stand on the side of the road in the direction you're going and yell out your destination if a taxi slows down or flashes its lights at you. If there are other passengers in the taxi, be sure to check the fare on the meter when you get in and calculate your own fare. The meter should read Fare 1 during the day, and Fare 2 from midnight to 5 a.m. or if you're traveling beyond the city limits. In large cities the fare is set by meter and in smaller places they may have a set fee to each location. If this is the case, there is a chart with the government-regulated fees in the taxi, and you should ask to see it if you feel the quoted price is too high. There are extra fees for luggage and to go to or from the airport, port, bus, or train stations. You can also reserve a taxi over the phone, either in advance or on the spot. Taxi company numbers are posted in the *Athens News*. Taxi drivers can either be wonderful conversationalists or notoriously rude, which may include smoking even though there is a no smoking sign displayed on the dashboard. Tipping is not expected, but people usually round up the fare.

Metro. The brand new *metro* in Athens is efficient and clean and is the best way of getting around the inner city. There are three lines, two new ones and an older one running from Piraeus to Kifissia via Omonia and Monsasteraki Squares where you can change to the other lines. The metro runs from 5 a.m. to 12 midnight.

On all public transportation be sure to validate and hold on to your ticket in case the control inspectors check. If you do not have a validated ticket, there is a steep fine.

Car Rentals. There are car rental companies at the airport, in the cities, and at all major tourist areas. For Americans, you should be able to use your American driver's license in theory, but sometimes you may be asked for an international driver's license. It's best to check with your travel agent or car rental company before coming to find out what the latest procedure is. Greece has the highest accident rate in Europe, so drive defensively.

Shopping

Shops generally open around 8:30 a.m. Many close for the mid-afternoon siesta (*to mesiméri*) from 2 p.m. to 5 p.m., and then open again until 8 p.m. or so. Most tourist shops in season are open all day and late into the evening.

Groceries. There are many large supermarkets and mini-markets all over Greece. You can find pretty much anything you want, including specialty products, at the supermarkets. The farmer's markets (see *Markets* on page 16) are the best place to buy seasonal fruit and vegetables, but supermarkets also have them. For the freshest meat, try to find a butcher with local (*dópia*) meat, or you can buy it at the supermarket.

Electronic Goods. CD players, TV's, VCR's, DVD players, computers, printers, and telephones are available in all big towns around Greece. North American videos run on a different system than those in Europe, but it's possible to get a VCR that plays both. If you bring your own electronic equipment, you'll need a converter for 220 voltage.

Home Furnishings. All large towns have home furnishing stores. Such items as furniture, lamps, kitchen items, irons, heaters are all easily found. You can also have customized furniture made in Greece, sometimes at a reasonable price. Sheets tend to be either cheap and shoddy or high quality and quite expensive, so many expats bring their own.

Clothing. There's a full range of clothing stores in Greece, from chic boutiques in Kolonaki and some tourist areas to inexpensive shops around Omonia Square or Piraeus. Ermou Street, between Syntagma and Monasteraki Squares, is also a major shopping street with both chic and inexpensive shops. There are not many "outlet" stores offering bargain prices. There is well-made Greek "tourist wear" (sweaters, linen or cotton pants and shirts, and sandals) available in all tourist areas. If you change your mind about a purchase, it may be difficult to return it for cash, although some places may let you make an exchange.

Sizing charts
comparing British, American, and Continental

Suits and Dresses:

British	8	10	12	14	16	18
American	4	6	8	10	12	14
Continental	36	38	40	42	44	46

Shoes:

British	4	5	6	7	8	9	10
American	5	6	7	8	9	10	11
Continental	37	38	39	40	41	42	43

Gypsy sellers. Gypsies ply their goods from village to village and have inexpensive clothing, sheets, chairs, pots and pans, etc. It is customary to bargain with them. They usually travel in trucks and announce their arrival and their wares on a loudspeaker. Some also sell vegetables, fruit, and live chickens.

Markets

Some of the main products of Greece that are exported to other European countries and beyond are olives and olive oil, yoghurt, cheese, pistachios, dried figs, capers, herbs, fish, wine, vegetables, and fruit. These items are plentiful in the markets all over Greece. Depending on the size of the town or village, there will most likely be an open-air market. Many of these are run by farmers selling their home grown products, and they operate in the morning. Athens and Thessaloniki have huge open-air markets open 6 days a week. The Athens market is located on Athinas Street between Omonia and Monasteraki Squares. Certain areas of Athens have a *laiki*, or traditional outdoor market, on a designated day each week. These are all lively events, with vendors shouting out the merits of their produce.

Some typical winter crops are carrots, lettuce, artichokes, apples, pomegranates, and citrus fruits. Summer crops are tomatoes, cucumbers, melons, peaches, grapes, zucchini, and figs. Nowadays with the prevalence of green houses, out of season fruit and vegetables are available. If you have a craving for "exotic" fruits and vegetables, like avocados, asparagus, mushrooms, kiwi, and bananas, these can also be found in some markets.

Athens also has a large flea market in the Monasteraki district. Sunday is the main market day with many itinerant vendors selling goods from the former Soviet bloc, antiques, clothes, used books, records, and hardware.

Kiosks (Períptera)

Kiosks are located in convenient spots in every town. These small wooden structures were originally given to wounded war veterans by the government to provide for their livelihood. They sell newspapers, magazines, cigarettes, drinks, sweets, and postcards along with an array of other things.

Health and Medical Care

There are no serious diseases in Greece that are not also typical of the rest of Europe and North America; immunizations are not needed to enter the country. The main health hazard you need to watch out for is sunstroke and sunburn. Be sure to wear a hat and sun-block. It is safe to drink tap water in most places in Greece, but there is also bottled water if you prefer.

Emergencies like broken bones and cuts are treated free, or for a small fee, at state hospitals in the out-patient department. However, a visit to the public hospital can be disconcerting. You may need to wait a long time, and the doctors tend to be under stress. Greeks tend to give the doctor a *fákalos* (envelope) with a "tip" for the doctor, since they are not well paid, and to assure good service. There are also private doctors and hospitals available for more attentive care. These doctors work for hospitals during the day, and usually have private office hours in the early evening. You will need to pay in cash. If you have insurance, be sure to get a receipt so the insurance company can reimburse you. Doctors are specialized in Greece, and it's easy to recognize the area of specialty since the English names come from the Greek. For example, *kardiológos* or *gynekológos*. A specialist in Internal Medicine, though, is called a *pathológos*.

Pharmacies (Farmakía)

Pharmacists in Greece are excellent and can suggest drugs for you if you have a minor ailment. You may not need a prescription to purchase medication in Greece as long as you can let the pharmacist know exactly what you need. However, any narcotics, like codeine for a cough, or psychotropic drugs require a prescription. Pharmaceuticals are much cheaper than in the U.S. There is a rotating pharmacy schedule in every town on weekends and holidays; if necessary, check your local paper or ask someone to help you find one.

Climate

Greece is sunny, hot, and dry in the summer, although the last few years the summers have been more humid than usual. On the islands there's a cool north wind called *meltémi*. The hot south wind, the *scirócco*, blows in from North Africa. By contrast, Greek winters can be rainy, windy, and very damp, although interspersed with sunny and warm days. Central heating is very rare in the older traditional type homes, so be prepared for a damp house if you choose to live in one, and you may want to bring a sleeping bag for the winter months. Electric heaters are available, but they're quite expensive to run. The spring, which starts around mid-April, and the fall, which runs into November, are brilliant weather-wise, and the best time to be in Greece.

Clothing

Appearances are important in Greece. Greeks tend to dress casually, but smartly, even in the cities at night. You'll need very warm clothing in winter. There are coin operated laundramats as well as laundry services that will do your washing for you in the larger towns. Clothing is usually hung out to dry, so on rainy winter days it may take a while to get your clothes back from the cleaners. Dry cleaners are also available, but expensive.

Security

Greece has always been a very safe country, with one of the lowest crime rates in Europe. However, crime has been on the increase lately, especially pick-pocketing on public transportation. Some precautions should be taken, as anywhere, but you don't need to be overly wary. And as in most places in the world today, there is always a fear of terrorism. The main local terrorist organization, *November 17*, has been arrested, but there are other anarchic groups. These will sometimes march on the American embassy.

Strikes *(Aporyía)*

Strikes are frequent in Greece. Some may go unnoticed by the foreigner, such as when teachers or other civil servants, or even doctors and lawyers strike. However, transportation strikes, meaning taxis and Olympic Airways, may be a problem. As this is being written, both public school teachers and university professors are striking for more money, the taxis just ended a 4-day strike protesting the use of new meters and to gain access to bus lanes, and Olympic Airways had a walk out last week leaving many travelers stranded.

Tipping

In restaurants, the government-regulated service charge is always included in the price of the bill. If you feel service has been extra good, you could leave an additional tip. Most restaurants and tavernas in tourist areas expect this additional tip. For taxis the bill can be rounded up, or you can add a bit extra if the service has been extra good. Hairdressers are also tipped about 5-10%.

Conversions

Like the rest of Europe, Greece uses the metric system. In the grocery store, cheese, meat, vegetables, and fruit are sold by grams or kilos. Useful phrases are *misókilo* (half kilo) and *éna tétarto* (1/4 kilo). While liquids such as milk and water are sold by liquid measure (liter), wine is weighed (kilo).

Measurements

Metric	U.S.

Weights and Linear

Metric	U.S.
1 gram (g)	0.035 ounce
28.35 grams	1 ounce
100 grams	3.5 ounces
454 grams	1 pound
1 kilogram ("kilo")	2.2 pounds
1 centimeter (cm.)	0.3937 inch
2.54 centimeters	1 inch
1 meter (m.)	3.280 feet
1609.3 meters	1 mile

Liquid Measures

Metric	U.S.
1 liter (l.)	4.226 cups
1 liter	2.113 pints
1 liter	1.056 quarts
3.785 liters	1 gallon

Dry Measures

Metric	U.S.
1 liter	0.908 quart
1 decaliter (10 l.)	1.135 pecks
1 hectoliter (100 l.)	2.837 bushels

Kitchen Equivalents

Metric	U.S.
200 grams	1 cup of sugar
150 grams	1 cup of flour
5 grams	1 tsp.
12 grams	1 tbsp.

Kilometers and Miles		Thermometer Readings*	
1 km	0.6 miles	38 C.	100.4 F
3	1.8	35	95
5	3.1	30	86
8	4.9	25	77
10	6.2	21	69.8
15	9.3	10	50
20	12.4	5	41
25	15.5	0	32
35	21.7	–5	23
50	31.0	–10	14
100	62.1	–15	5
200	124.2	–17	1.4
300	186.4	–25	–13
500	310.6	–30	–22

*European thermometers use the centigrade scale. To convert Fahrenheit to centigrade, subtract 32, then multiply by 5 and divide by 9. To convert centigrade to Fahrenheit, multiply by 9, divide by 5 and add 32. The chart above gives an approximate conversion.

Electricity

Electricity is 220 volts with a round prong plug. For North Americans, if you do not have dual voltage on your hair dryer, cassette player, shaver, or computer you will need a converter and an adapter. If possible, bring equipment with dual voltage and then just use an adapter plug.

Pets

There are many stray cats and dogs in Greece, which are fed by people in the neighborhood. Leftovers are left in a convenient place for these strays. Tourists sometimes adopt an animal during their stay, and then leave them to fend for themselves once they leave Greece. Cats, for instance, lose their ability to survive in the wild after they've been adopted. If you decide to adopt a pet, care should be taken that its welfare is provided for after you are gone. If you fall in love with a dog or cat, you can quite easily bring it home with you by getting the proper shots and documents.

Leisure Activities

Reading. All the latest books can be found in major cities and tourist areas, as well as the airport. Expats are generous about sharing their books, and book clubs exist wherever there is a large community of foreigners.

Cinema. All cities and large towns have movie theaters. American movies generally play two months or so after playing in the U.S., and all movies are shown in the original language with Greek subtitles. The schedules for the cinemas in Athens are listed in *The Athens News*. In smaller towns and tourist areas announcements are posted around town. There are open-air cinemas during the summer, where you can sit at a table outside and have a cheese pie and drink an ouzo while watching the movie. Thessaloniki has an international film festival in October.

Video and DVD Rentals. All large cities have video rental shops at reasonable prices.

Cultural Life

Theater and Opera. Athens has around 45 theaters operating from September to May with most productions in Greek. There is also an opera house on Akadhimas Street in central Athens. In summer classical Greek plays are performed in ancient theaters in Epidauros and Athens. The English language newspapers have listings.

Megaron Musikis. In winter the Megaron Musikis, on Vassilias Sofias near the American Embassy, has quality symphony, opera, and other performances from all over the world.

Athens Festival. In summer there are shows (opera, theater, music) in outdoor theaters around the city. The Irodian, an ancient Roman theater with a view of the Acropolis, or Lykavitos Hill, overlooking Athens, are two of the best.

Museums and Archaeological Sites

Most museums and archaeological sites are open every day except Monday. Entrance fees vary depending on the site and are free on Sunday during the winter months. Newspapers and tourist offices have information on each site in their area. It is strictly forbidden to take away artifacts, including pottery shards, from archaeological sites.

Nightlife

Clubbing is very popular throughout the country. You can find everything from discos to Greek music, or from techno to Latin. They usually start after midnight and go till early morning. Some specialty clubs also serve food. In summer many clubs are outside near the sea. The entrance fee can be quite hefty and includes the first drink. Additional drinks are more expensive than at a regular bar.

Bars of all types are plentiful around the country. Some have music and a dance floor, and others are just for a quiet drink.

Bouzoukia are the typical Greek entertainment and start around midnight with the *bouzouki*, a mandolin-like instrument, as the featured instrument. Greeks go to the *bouzoukia* with their *paréa* (see page 46). Usually a bottle of whisky and mixers are ordered for everyone to share. It is an excellent way to see Greek dancing. There are a few etiquette rules in a *bouzouki* bar. Dances are requested by tossing money at the band. If those who pay get up and dance, it is "their song," and it may be bad form to join in, unless you are invited. Line dances, like the *sirtó* and *hassipisérviko* (see *Dances* on page 74) are usually open to anyone. In a line dance, you should not take the lead, unless you are invited to by the person leading. If you want to join a line dance you should hook up at the end, or if it's too crowded, break in at the middle.

Sports

Water Sports. Windsurfers can be rented at most tourist beaches. Water-skiing is less popular but available in some places. Snorkeling and scuba diving are popular in Greece. Yachts and sailboats can be rented if there are two people on board with their captain's licenses, or rented with a crew if you don't sail yourselves.

Land Sports. Golf isn't widely played in Greece except at a few courses near Athens, Thessaloniki, and Crete. There are tennis courts near the large cities and tourist areas.

Skiing. You can ski from December to March in the north at places like Grevena in Macedonia, Mt. Parnithos near Athens, or Kalavrita in the Peloponnese. The cost of renting equipment and the lift ticket are very reasonable. Alpine, cross-country skiing, and snowboarding are all popular, although snow conditions and facilities vary from resort to resort. Check the internet for the latest information.

Hiking and mountain climbing are wonderful all over Greece. There are many donkey paths throughout the country, which make good hiking trails. Many of them are marked by blue, red, or yellow dots on stones (courtesy of various hiking groups). You can make a good hiking excursion from village to village, in gorges in Crete and Epirus, or to remote monasteries. There are some good hiking maps of various areas in Greece.

Bicycling. You can rent bicycles in the tourist areas, or bring your own. A word of caution – it can be very hilly, and the traffic can be dangerous or even harrowing. Bicycle riding is not a common mode of transportation, except in some places like Kos or Larissa where it is flat.

Fishing is extremely popular. You can purchase a bamboo pole with line and hook and cast away. Greeks love other fisher-people and will offer you lots of advice on what you need to do. Spear fishing is also popular.

Team Sports. Basketball and soccer are the two most widely played and avidly watched team sports in Greece. There is a movement afoot to get Greeks involved with baseball promoted by a Greek American baseball player.

Finding a Place to Live

English newspapers, such as *The Athens News* or the Greek paper *Chrisi Efkairia*, are good places to start your search for a place to live in Athens. Another method, if you know which part of town you'd like to live in, is to wander around looking for yellow *"Enoikiazete"* (For Rent) signs. There are also real estate agents, but you may want to check their credentials, as well as determine the fee. You should check around to find out what a proper monthly rental should be based on length of stay, location, type of accommodation, and time of year. You can sometimes negotiate the asked-for rental price. Make sure it is clear what expenses will be your responsibility. For instance, you may have to pay "common fees" in apartment buildings, and these can sometimes raise the rent as much as 10%. If possible, this should all be set out in a contract. Central heating, if you have it, may need to be supplemented with a portable gas or electric heater. Electricity is cheaper to run at night.

Unless you rent a furnished apartment, apartments come completely bare, meaning there won't be a refrigerator or stove. You should make sure the apartment is thoroughly cleaned and painted before you move in. You may be required to pay two or three months rent when you sign the contract. On islands or in smaller towns, the best way to find a house or apartment is to ask people if they know of an available place to live in your chosen neighborhood.

Paying Bills

The two most common bills for renters are telephone and electricity, although you may have a water bill, too. These bills come every two months and must be paid in person, in cash. Most bills can be paid at the post office, or other convenient spots. The telephone bills show the number of units (*monádhes*) used and only lately have become itemized in some places. The electricity meter is read 3 times per year, so your bill may be an estimate based on the last year's usage. The corrected bill will arrive the next time after the meter has been read.

Residence Visas and Work Permits

The following applies to non-EU nationals. For citizens of the EU, Greece follows the same rules as the rest of the Union.

Most non-EU Western nationals are given a three-month tourist visa when they enter Greece. This can be extended (there is a fee) an additional three months quite easily. Be prepared for bureaucratic delays, and start applying no later than 2 weeks before expiration of your tourist visa. If financial solvency can be shown, you may even be able to get a third 3-month extension. You may be asked to produce your traveler's checks, credit cards, or Greek bankbooks as proof. One reason for such scrutiny is to make sure that you are not working illegally. After that you will have to leave the EU countries for 3 months. Should you fail to apply for an extension and stay over your tourist visa or extension, you may be fined on departure. However, you will not need to go through passport control in Greece if you travel to another Schengen country (most EU countries, but not England). If you're flying directly to a non-Schengen country (directly to New York for example), you will go through passport control.

If you are studying in Greece, you should be able to get a student visa for the length of your studies. You should check with the Greek consulate or embassy before coming to find out the latest procedure, but beware that they themselves often don't know! The best procedure is to double check all information you receive. The American Embassy in Athens is a good source for visa regulations for North Americans (www.usembassy.gr)

It's also possible to get a residence visa, which allows you to stay in Greece for up to a year, if you have a work permit. This can be extended as long as you are still working legally. Work permits need to be applied for by your employer and must be obtained before you enter the country. It is an extremely long and arduous process to get a work permit for a non-EU citizen, but it can be done. The first thing is you have to have an employer willing to go to the trouble. Once you have a work permit you must get it extended every year as long as you are still working. Working in Greece means paying taxes, so you will need a tax number (AFM), you will also need a contract for your apartment, and the phone and electricity in your name (you may be asked to produce these bills at the bureaucracy). It also means you will pay into and be entitled to the Greek health care system (IKA). The all-important IKA stamps as well as tax-filing declaration must be shown each year to renew your residence and work permits.

It is also possible, if you are self-employed, to work out a scheme where you pay your own IKA. Laws for residence visas and work permits change all the time, so be sure to double-check what the latest rulings are.

Picking up Work

If you want to try winging it on your tourist visa, the following jobs can be found:

Teaching English. Frontistíria, private language institutes, exist in every large town. Most students attend *frontistíria* in order to pass the Cambridge or Michigan exams to get level certification in English. The requirement for a native speaker of English to work at a *frontistíria* is any BA or BS university degree (bring a copy of your diploma and transcript with you). If you have a certificate or a graduate degree in TEFL, your chances of finding work will increase.

Jobs are easy to find on the spot. Once you have decided on the place you would like to stay, go around to the *frontistíria* in that community. Hiring is done in August and September for the year, and sometimes again in January. You can also check the classifieds in *The Athens News.* Great emphasis will be placed on your appearance and the rapport you establish with the director.

You should check on the credibility and reliability of any *frontisitíria* you are considering. Wages vary from place to place. Pay is quite low, but is enough to live on, especially if supplemented with private lessons, which can be quite lucrative. You will be paid for the hours you actually work, and will most likely not be paid during holidays, although Christmas and Easter bonuses are the norm. There are usually 25 to 30 teaching hours per week in the afternoons and early evenings and on Saturdays.

Tourist work. It is also possible to find work in tourist areas, at hotels, restaurants, bars, travel agencies, and shops. Again, the best way to find these jobs is by asking around at the beginning of the season (around Easter). If you come from a non-EU country, you will need to work out your own arrangements to stay in the country beyond the 3-month tourist visa. Expect to work long hours, seven days a week.

Customs and Values

Caveat

Traditional Greek culture is changing at a very rapid pace. Some of the instances given below concerning cultural aspects are traditional but no longer typically true. The changes are most prevalent in the cities, in particular in Athens. The provinces are more conservative and may retain more of the traditional values and customs. Yet it's important in understanding the Greek character to have some knowledge of what their traditional culture was like for centuries and the lingering influence it still has in its modified form today.

The Village

For centuries Greece was an agricultural and rural society. Day to day rhythms revolved around the agricultural season and religious holidays. The hub of village life was the main square (*platía*) and the *cafenío* where men gathered. The roles of men and women were firmly established. Essentially the men were in charge of public life and the women of the home. There was both cooperation and conflict in the village. Cooperation was established through family ties and *koumbáros*, that is by being the godparent of an unrelated family or the best man at a wedding. The most extreme examples of conflict were the vendettas, sometimes running for centuries, in Crete and in the Mani, the middle peninsula in the southern Peloponnese.

Today there is a tendency to move to the cities, for work, study, and status. Residents of the provinces often have an apartment in Athens or Thessaloniki. Even with this exodus to the cities, Greeks still feel a strong connection to their village (*xorió*). There is a strong sense of local pride and an identification with one's village, and many city dwellers return for the major holidays and summer. Neighborhoods in the cities are often village based, people from the same village now living in the same neighborhood (*gítonas*). This was even true with emigrants to the United States, where, for example, Mykonians settled in Joliette, Illinois, and Kalymnians in Tarpon Springs, Florida.

Cafeníos

These traditional coffee houses are centrally located in the main square (*platía*) of every village, and they were the hub of village life. They are frequently crowded with men smoking, drinking coffee, playing cards or backgammon (*távli*), and discussing the latest events. Groups of men socialize together in their *paréa*, and the main ethos or spirit of the cafenío is that of *kerásma* or treating one another. (See *Greek Cultural Terms* on page 45.) In the villages, the custom of going to the cafenío is traditionally for men only. Greek women rarely enter, although this prohibition is not as strict these days as in the past.

Family Life

Families are a close economic unit in Greece, and all members contribute to the advancement of the family. They are affectionately involved with one another; for example, family members call each other several times a day, a practice that has been made easier by the ever-present cell phone. Children tend to live with their parents until they are married, no matter what age they are. Traditionally the father provided for the economic needs of the family and disciplined the children, and the mother took care of the home and raising the children. In some communities the women also helped with the farm work, in addition to selling farm products such as eggs and cheese in market (*pazári*). Nowadays, many women have careers, yet they still take care of the housework.

Because it is each family member's obligation to contribute to the family welfare, earnings go into the family pool in many cases. There is not an assumption of economic independence from the family. Children usually provide for their elderly parents (especially if one of them is widowed) so it is very common to have grandparents living with them. The grandmother *(yía-yía)* may take an active role in the upbringing of children and helps instill the traditional values in family life.

Traditionally most marriages were arranged *(proxenió)* to the mutual economic benefit of both families. Marriage was considered an alliance between two families. The bride's family provided a dowry *(príka)*. The amount of the *príka* was negotiated between the two families, but nearly always included a house, as well as money, fields, and things for the home. If a house was not provided, the newlyweds would live with their in-laws (usually paternal). In the past, brothers did not marry until their sisters had been dowered and married. The dowry system is no longer required according to the Family Law Revisions of 1984, although the bride's parents sometimes still provide a house for the couple to live in, especially in the countryside. Nowadays, dating is very common and most couples choose their partners. Civil marriages, outside the church, are allowed since the Family Law revisions. The law also allows for divorce by mutual consent.

Socialization occurs within the family, as it does everywhere. Children are constantly talked to and pick up their conversational skills this way. They are often taught to be wary of those outside of the family circle and to acquire a cunning intelligence. There is a rather cavalier approach to disciplining children. Stubbornness or manipulative behavior may be grudgingly admired as showing character. Children often go out with their parents in the evening to tavernas or cultural events and are generally given free run of the place.

Religion

Ninety-seven percent of the population of Greece is Greek Orthodox. Greek Orthodoxy permeates Greek life and in most cases is synonymous with being Greek. Mykonos, a small island, claims to have over 365 churches. Churches and chapels dot the countryside everywhere, and range in size from the small and simple to the enormous and ornate. Families who can afford it build their own churches, sometimes to fulfill a promise to a saint who has helped them, and each church is named after a saint. Icons of saints, painted on wood and embellished with gold or silver are liberally displayed in all churches.

The Orthodox services are elaborate and ritualistic. When the wor-shipers arrive in church, they light candles and kiss icons. The smell of incense fills the air. People come and go at will, or may even have a brief chat. Most people stand in the church, although there are a few chairs along the sides for older people. There is some segregation by sex, usually with the men in the center and the women along the sides. The priest performs the liturgy and cantors sing Byzantine chants. The liturgy is recited in *koíne* Greek (see *The Greek Language* on page 75), so it is not entirely understood by all attending; this is similar to the way Latin used to be in the Catholic church. The high point of the service is the mystery of the Holy Eucharist. The "mysteries" are located in back of the *iconostasis* (wall of icons) behind the altar. Women are for-bidden to enter this part of the church. Greek women do not take Com-munion or kiss icons when they have their periods. As part of their involvement in the life of their church, Greeks who can afford it do-nate the food for the *Paniyíri* (festivals) or contribute to the white-washing of the church.

The early Christian church split into the Orthodox and Roman Catholic churches in 1054 (see 'History, Byzantium' for reasons why). Some of the noticeable differences between the two are that in the Orthodox faith priests can marry and leavened bread is used in the celebration of the Eucharist. Icons, rather than statues, depict the holy family and saints. Icons are found not only in churches, but in homes as well. Easter is the most important holiday in both the Orthodox and Roman Catholic traditions. In Orthodoxy, however, because of the importance of the resurrection, Christ is usually portrayed gloriously rising from death, rather than dying on the cross.

The veneration of saints (*áyios* - masculine saint; *áyia* - feminine) is important in both the Orthodox and Catholic churches. They have some of the early saints in common, but ever since the schism they have each adopted new ones. Therefore, many saints who have been central to the Catholic faith, for instance St. Augustine and St. Francis, are not part of the Orthodox tradition. In times of need, Greeks pray to their saints. Since they each have their own attributes, the choice of which saint to call on depends on the circumstances.

One typically Greek saint is St. Pareskaví who heals those with eye problems. Those in need may place silver amulets (*támata*) with a design of an eye, on her icon. The most recent Greek saint is St. Nektarios who lived in the 19th century on the island of Aegina. Some of the Greek saints have clearly assumed some of the attributes of the old polytheistic Greek gods. Much like Zeus, the Prophet Elijah (*Ilías*) is the saint of rain, wind, lightning, and thunder. The churches dedicated to Ilias are found on hilltops. Saint Nicholas rules the seas, like Poseidon, and protects seamen. Many churches dedicated to St. Nicholas are near the sea, and seamen carry his icon on their boats.

What's in a Name

Most Greeks are named after saints. Traditionally, Greeks celebrated their saint's name day rather than their birthdays; nowadays birthdays are also celebrated. It is customary to name the first born children in a family after the paternal grandparents and subsequent children after the maternal grandparents. This way the same names are carried on through the generations. In Greece your middle name is your father's first name. Your last name is your family name, but the ending of your last name changes if you're male or female. So Maria Stavros Georgopoulou and Manolis Stavros Georgopoulos are brother and sister and the children of Stavros. Their grandparents probably had the names Maria and Manolis.

You can also sometimes tell where a person is from by the ending of their last name: "-akis" tend to be from Crete, "-opoulos" are originally from the Peloponnese, "-idhis" are Black Sea Greeks (*Póntos*), and "-glou" from Asia Minor. As with English names like Smith, Weaver, Cooper, and Clark, Greeks were sometimes given names based on their family business such as Papayiannis, who would have been "Father John," or Kanistras, someone who made baskets. Names are also descriptive such as Mavroyiannis (Black John) or Xanthi (Blonde). "Chatzi" followed by a name, such as Chatzimichalis, means their ancestor, Michalis, made the "haj" to Jerusalem.

Name Day Celebrations (*Eortís*)

Churches are named after saints, and on that saint's day there is a liturgy at that church. This is followed by a religious feast (*Paniyíri*) for members of the community. The food might consist of beans, bread, olives, and wine or can be quite lavish with fish or meat. *Paniyíri* is an ancient Greek word meaning "all those gathered in a public place" – (*pan agora*) "across/spanning the marketplace." These festivals were originally held in ancient Greece to honor the gods and goddesses; now it's the saints who are honored. This is one of the many examples of the Christianization of former pagan rites.

On St. Nicholas Day, December 6th, the bells toll and the liturgy begins early in the morning at churches called St. Nicholas. Around 10 a.m. there is a procession through the churchyard or the village. The priests and some male members of the community lead the procession carrying the icon of St. Nicholas. Scented holy water is sprinkled on the assembled worshipers. Generally, around 10:30 the *Paniyíri* begins. The food and wine is consumed as everyone mills around the churchyard socializing, or sitting in a special church-yard dining area. If it's an especially prominent name day in the community, musicians may come by, the wine flows, and there is dancing all day long. Foreigners shouldn't be shy about joining in the *paniyíri*. Since people come and go all day, it's also all right to arrive late.

It is customary to visit your friend's home on their name day to wish them "*chrónia pollá*" (many years) and bring a gift. Typical gifts are candy, flowers, or whiskey; or if you're close friends, something more personal. You will be offered a sweet, coffee or liquor, or food all served with the utmost attention. If the name day party is held in a restaurant, celebrants always treat their friends.

Rites of Passage

Baptism *(Váftisma)* Greek babies are called "baby" *(bébis* (M) or *béba* (F)) until the baptism, traditionally 40 days after birth. In the past the mother would not leave the house for 40 days after birth to avoid the *máyia,* or evil spirits. Nowadays, the baptism is anytime after the 40-day period up to toddler age. The *koumbáros* (godfather) baptizes and names the baby. The priest faces the baby eastward (towards Jerusalem) and blows three times to chase away evil spirits. The *koumbáros* then rubs olive oil over the baby's naked body and the priest dunks the baby three times into the bathtub-size font. The priest cuts three small locks of the baby's hair as a gift to Christ and then holds the baby up to the altar three times. The "three" in these rituals symbolizes the Holy Trinity. Baptism, communion, and confirmation are all performed at this one time.

Common expressions at baptisms are: *"Na sas zísi"* (Life to the parents, godparents, etc.) or *"Na zisi"* (May s/he live). The greeting for the godparents is *"Pánta axioi"* (May you always be able, the implication is "to fulfill your duty as a godparent.") *Boubouníeres,* small decorative packets with sugar coated almonds are handed out after the ceremony. Close friends go the parent's home or a taverna for the celebration of the blessed event.

Weddings *(Gámos)* Traditionally there was an official engagement period when the marriage was announced to the community, at which time the couple could be seen in public together. This engagement was blessed by the priest and wedding bands were exchanged which were worn on the left hand (the right after marriage.) The traditional engagement wish is *"Sigcharitiria"* (Congratulations). Nowadays, engagements tend to be less prescribed.

A few days before the wedding, friends get together at the nuptial home for the ritual bedmaking *(to kreváti).* All the single women make the bridal bed while the married women sing for the couple's early and prosperous marriage. The priest blesses the bed and the guests toss money onto it. Sometimes they also toss rice (symbolizing a long life together), sugar coated almonds (for happiness and a "sweet life"), and flowers (for beauty). Then a baby may be put on the bed to symbolize fertility.

33

On the wedding day the bridal party goes to the bride's home to collect her. Nowadays they usually drive to the church, but traditionally they walked in a procession often accompanied by musicians. The guests follow the couple into the church and everyone stands during the ceremony. The priest blesses the wedding rings and places them on their right hands, the *koumbáros*, the best man, exchanges them three times between the bride and groom. Wedding crowns, *stéfana*, are placed on the bridal couple's heads by the priest and then exchanged three times by the *koumbáros*, followed by three sips of wine. Next they walk around the altar three times, in the "Dance of Isaiah," while being pelted with rice and flowers. There is a receiving line at the church when *boubouníera* are handed out. The ceremony is usually followed by a lavish reception at a restaurant

A greeting before the wedding is *"I óra kalí"* (The time is good), or *"Kala stéfana"* ("Good wreaths", referring to the wreaths which crown the bridal couple.) At the wedding it is common to say, *"Na Zísete"* referring to a good life together; or *"Vío Andhospárto"* which means a life full of children.

Funerals (Kidia) In the villages, the traditional funeral, which is described here, still takes place. The funeral is held the day after death, if possible. When someone dies in a village, the church bells toll the death knell. Black rimmed notices are put up around the village, announcing the death. It is very important that family members and friends watch over the body until burial to keep the devil away. Mirrors are covered, and a plate is placed under the coffin. The plate is broken when the body is taken to the church. In the past, in some places such as Mykonos, the Mani peninsula, and Thessaly, mourners sang dirges, *mirolóyia*, recounting the events and successes in the deceased person's life. The body may be carried in an open casket through the village to the church for the service and then to the cemetery for burial. Usual condolences at funerals are *"Zoi se sas"* (Life to you) or *"Silipitíria"* (Condolences). Nowadays, at least in the cities, funerals are not usually held at home.

A photograph of the deceased and flowers are placed on the grave, and lovingly and attentively cared for by family members. Male relatives wear a black armband for 40 days. In the past, widows wore black for the rest of their lives and did not remarry. It is believed that the soul lingers for three days before being released from the body at which time there is a ceremony at the grave with family members.

Forty days later the soul ascends to heaven at which time there is a special liturgy at the church. Thereafter there are remembrance liturgies on the annual anniversaries of death. On these occasions a special boiled wheat mixture, *kólliva*, is prepared using different types of grain which are cleaned three times by three different women. The cake is then elaborately decorated with icing and silver sugar pellets and distributed to the attendees of the memorial service along with a sip of brandy. After a time, but no sooner than the third year, the body is exhumed. If there is skin left on the bones, it is believed that the person had difficulty getting to heaven. The bones are washed and placed in an urn in the family crypt. There is a photograph of the deceased placed near the urn. In the Orthodox Church and in Greece, Cremation is forbidden.

Festivals

The starred (*) holidays are public religious holidays. There are also two secular public holidays:

*New Year's Day *(St. Vasílios' Day).* St. Vasílios (Basil) is the Greek Santa Claus; children receive presents on this day. A special New Year sweet bread, *vassilópita,* is baked with a coin inside. The cake is distributed with the first piece going to St. Vasílios, then one for the house, then to each family member. There may also be slices for the poor or, in some villages, even for the animals. The person who gets the slice with the coin will be lucky throughout the year. The New Year's greeting is *"Kalí Chronía."*

*Epiphany *(January 6)* On Epiphany the waters are blessed by the priest. The priest casts a cross into the water and young men dive for it. The one who recovers the cross is the hero for the day. There is a *Paniyíri* following the blessing of the waters. Around Epiphany, priests go from house to house blessing the homes in their community.

Carnival (Apókries) Carnival festivities last for the three weeks leading up to Lent. There are masquerade parties and lots of merrymaking and feasting, and in the final days, there are parades. The biggest carnival celebration is in Patras. The greeting is *"Kalí Sarakósti"* (good lent).

*Clean Monday (Kathará Dheftéra) On this first day of Lent, most families go to the countryside for a picnic and to fly kites. Children will have made or bought kites, during the days leading up to Clean Monday. Only Lenten food can be eaten such as fish-roe salad *(taramasaláta)*, greens *(chórta), kalamari,* and *halva.* An unleavened bread, *lagána,* only baked on this day, is sold at the bakeries in the morning.

Maundy Thursday The week leading up to Easter is called *Megáli Efdhomádha* or Big Week. On Maundy Thursday eggs are dyed red for Easter Sunday morning, symbolizing the blood of Christ, and Christ's funeral bier, *Epitáfios,* is made from flowers gathered by women and children. The pre-Easter greeting is *"Kaló Páska."*

*Good Friday (Megáli Paraskaví) Offices are closed, flags are hung at half mast, and church bells toll the funeral knell. There is a sense of gloom everywhere. Fasting is observed in earnest on this day. Church services are held in the evening. At the end of the service, there is a solemn procession through town with pall bearers carrying the *epitáfios* and icons, followed by the worshipers mourning the death of Christ. The way is lit by candles and lights from homes along the path.

*Easter Saturday The paschal lamb or goat is usually slaughtered and prepared on this day. Easter services honoring the resurrection begin around 10 p.m. Just before midnight, the church is darkened and the congregation waits in silence, each holding an unlit candle. At the stroke of midnight, the priest lights the first candle from the perpetual light in the inner sanctum of the church and, as he offers the flame to the worshipers, he says: "Come and take the never-setting light and glorify Christ who has risen from the dead." The congregation solemnly light their candles one from each other and say: *"Christós anésti"* (Christ has risen) and then respond with: *"Alíthos anésti"* (He has truly risen). The church bells ring joyfully and homemade firecrackers are set off outside. It is good luck to walk home without your candle blowing out. Be careful of the firecrackers.

When the family gets home, their fast is broken with *mayerítsa,* a special soup made of lamb's lungs, intestines, and heart with an egg-lemon base. The red eggs are struck one against the other. The one whose egg doesn't crack is the winner. There are techniques to accomplish this.

Easter Sunday (Páska) The lamb or goat, along with a *kokorétsi* (lamb innards on a skewer and wrapped in intestines) are spit-roasted all day long. Everyone is in a festive mood while preparing the table and waiting for the lamb to cook. There is a special sweet bread called *lambrópsomo* with a red egg on top. For a few days after Easter the greetings are *"Christós anésti"* and *"Chrónia Pollá."* Orthodox Easter rarely falls on the same day as western Easter. Like western Easter, it is calculated as the Sunday after the full moon following the spring equinox; however, it must fall after the date of the celebration of Passover (The Last Supper).

St. George (Apr. 23) St. George is the patron saint of shepherds. For farmers this day marks the beginning of summer. If it falls during Lent, it is celebrated on Easter Monday.

May Day (May 1) Flowers are gathered in the countryside to make wreaths which are hung on doors. It has its roots in pre-Christian times and represents the change from winter to summer.

Dormition of the Virgin Mary (*August 15*) Pilgrimages are made to the church of St. Mary (*Evangelistria*) on the island of Tinos. This church has a famous icon of the Virgin Mary painted by St. Luke. It is believed this icon works miracles and can cure illnesses. It is covered with offerings such as jewelry or *tamáta*. Crutches and so forth have been left behind by those that were cured on the spot.

St. Demetrius (*October 26*) Demetrius is the patron saint of Thessaloniki. For farmers this day marks the beginning of the winter season. The new wine is opened on this day.

Christmas (*Christoúyena*) In Greece, Christmas is not as important as Easter. However, some traditions have been adopted from the west. Now homes are decorated with trees and lights, and sometimes gifts are exchanged. Traditionally there is no Santa Claus associated with Christmas. Instead, the Greeks have St. Vasílios, whose saints day is on New Year's Day (see above.) A special Christmas sweet bread, the *christópsomo* is decorated with a cross. Children go from house to house from Christmas to New Years singing carols (*kálanda*) for which they are given coins and sweets. The Christmas greeting is "*Kalá Christoúyena.*"

In addition to these main Orthodox festivals, there are countless saints' days throughout the year. Most calendars and agendas available in Greece list them.

National Holidays

Independence Day (March 25) celebrates the anniversary of the uprising against the Turks in 1821. There are parades in most towns.

Ochi Day (October 28) In 1940, Italy, backed by Hitler, demanded the surrender of Greece to the Italian army. General Ioannis Metaxas said, "*Ochi!*" "No!" Greece sided with the Allies, for some time as Britain's only surviving ally in Europe. Later they drove the Italians out of most of Albania and thwarted Hitler's paratrooper invasion of Crete. Although Greece was eventually overrun by the vast German and Italian armies, Greek resistance disrupted the Axis powers' plans, delayed the invasion of Russia, and thus began the end of the great war. With its brutal supression, Greece paid a terrible price. To commemorate the anniversary of Metaxas' brave "*Ochi!*" military parades are held in major cities and services in many churches around the country.

Cross-Cultural Issues

Contradictions in Character

Greekness is not easy to pigeonhole, and for every truth there's an opposing one. Greeks are highly individualistic, yet at the same time very group-oriented when it comes to their families. They can be trusting, but also suspicious. They can be warmhearted and generous or selfish and cunning. They can be a combination of the traditional and modern. For just about every character trait you'll meet, you'll also meet the opposite. You may even find conflicting character traits in the same person, depending on your relationship with an individual.

One important factor that has determined the Greek character is their long and varied history. For example, they are very sensitive to outside interference in their national affairs, which may be a result of the long years of Ottoman domination. Another determining factor in the Greek character is their connection to their villages. Most Greeks have long ago left their villages and moved to the cities, but they've kept close ties there, and visit on holidays. (See *The Village* on page 27.)

Greetings

Greeks are gregarious and like to greet their friends in the street. The most common greeting is: "Hello! How are you?" - "*Yiá sou! Ti Kánis;*" (the semi-colon is the question mark in Greek). The response is "Fine, and you?" "*Kalá, k'esí;*" Close friends and relatives, both men and women, kiss each other once on each cheek when they meet, especially if some time has passed since they last met. Shaking hands is also common.

The Greek language has both an informal and a formal form. Like French and German, the formal is the second person plural. The informal, *Yiá sou*, is the most common expression used for both greeting and leave-taking for one person you know well; it literally means "health to you." The formal form, also used for greeting more than one person, is the plural, *yiá sas*. The formal is generally used when talking with older people, priests, most strangers, or people in high position. A general rule of thumb is, if you are addressed in the formal form, then it should be used in return. For other polite expressions, see *Some Useful Expressions* on page 85.

In the countryside, Greeks may be friendly towards foreigners, so strangers may greet you on country roads. They may call out "Good day," "*Chérete*." Good morning is "*Káli méra*" and the formal is "*Káli mérasas.*"

When introduced to someone for the first time you should shake hands, and say: "I am very glad (to meet you) Mrs. Kavalari" "*Cháro polí kíria Kavalári.*" The response is "Same to you," "*Epísis.*"

Conversation

Conversation (*kouvénda*) is a way of life in Greece. It is a form of amusement and a way of passing the time. Everywhere you go— cafes, restaurants, homes, even churches, people are abuzz, animatedly debating the pros and cons of the latest political happenings or hashing over the latest gossip. Nothing seems too inconsequential to be deliberated at great length by one and all, and everyone has their own opinion on the issue at hand.

Spontaneity is highly valued in Greek society. Greeks have a healthy thirst for life and a natural curiosity about the world. They may think nothing of asking questions that may be considered taboo to some. On your first encounter with someone, you may be asked how old you are, whether or not you are married, or how much money you make. These questions are considered essential pieces of knowledge in order to get to know you. This is especially true with older people in the villages; urban Greeks and young people nowadays generally avoid these kinds of questions.

Communication Style

The Greek communication style could be called "high involvement." This can seem loud, combative, and emotional; everyone wants to share their opinion, and they're totally engaged in the conversation at hand. You may overhear a conversation and think a fight is about to break out, only to discover they're just discussing the weather. These kinds of argumentative exchanges often end with the speakers walking off arm-in-arm. The stereotype that Greeks are "loud" or "too emotional" comes from this high involvement communication style.

Gestures

As part of their the highly involved communication style, Greeks use numerous expressive gestures. The entire body takes part in the conversation, especially the face, hands, arms, and shoulders. Almost every verbal expression, such as delight or frustration, is accompanied by its correlating body movement; most Greeks never speak with their hands in their pockets. For instance, without a spoken word whole conversations can take place between the drivers of two different cars.

The Greek way of gesturing "no" and "yes" can be confusing to North Americans and others. The way one says "no" (*óchi*) is to throw your head back (which can be mistaken for a nod of agreement) and click your tongue against your teeth, with a lift of the eyebrows. This may seem like a disdainful gesture, arrogantly sticking your nose in the air. It isn't intended to be. Oftentimes *óchi* is expressed with just a slight lift of the eyebrows, so you have to pay close attention. The gesture for "yes" is to lower the head slightly and nod it once to the left; sometimes taken to be a quick, negative shake of the head. It is useful to adopt the click of the tongue and imperceptible lift of the eyebrows if pushy touts persist in trying to get you to go into their shop. It works wonders if you don't want to be hassled. In fact, this gesture works, with slight variations, in all the countries of the Mediterranean.

The most disparaging gesture among Greeks themselves is the uniquely Greek "*moútza*," which means something like "go to hell." This is done by holding the hand out straight with the five fingers extended (an exaggerated "Hi!" gesture). For added emphasis, "Na!" can be shouted at the same time. It has a huge impact on the recipient and is not recommended. Greeks frequently use it themselves on the road when they are irritated with other drivers.

Some other Greek gestures are: "I don't know" - shoulders raised, arms bent and palms held outward with an exaggerated frown on your face; "What's happening?"– a quick twist of the right hand to an upward facing position with fingers slightly spread and cupped; "You ought to be spanked" – right hand in a chopping motion while saying "*Thá fás xílo*" (You will eat wood); "Can you believe it?" or "Oh no."– right arm bent with right hand circling in a counterclockwise motion, head shaken with a slight frown while saying, "*Po, po, po*."

Time

Edward T. Hall has coined the terms polychronic and monochronic to classify time as a form of non-verbal communication in cultures. Monochronic cultures (like the U.S.) compartmentalize time, emphasize schedules and promptness, and usually only one person speaks at a time. Monochronic cultures view time as money and tend to be "tied to the clock." Care is taken to use time as efficiently as possible, it must not be "wasted."

Greece is a polychronic culture, which is characterized by many things happening at once. There are many people talking at the same time with constant interruptions, and the Greeks cope easily with this. In business offices, people knock on a door and walk in and state their business, even if it means interrupting an on-going conversation, and all the while the telephone may ring. Advance planning can sometimes be problematic, since many emergencies spring up at a moment's notice. Greeks tend to do things at the last minute, and usually manage to get it done.

In polychronic cultures, human relations are valued more than promptness and adhering to schedules. Traditionally, time was something to "pass."*Passatempos* (pumpkin seeds) are a snack traditionally munched on just to pass the time in the cafenío.

One of the joys of living in Greece is the pace of life – outside of Athens, that is – which is much slower than in other Western countries. Once you have adjusted to it, it can be quite enjoyable. You just can't expect that things will happen as quickly or efficiently as you might be used to.

Personal Space

Greeks stand closer together during conversation and very often touch each other much more than in some other Western countries. Again, this is related to the level of involvement in communication. The "personal bubble" of space, which seems right to some is much smaller in Greece. The bus door opens and everyone piles in helter-skelter with lots of pushing and shoving. Foreigners, and Greeks alike, who try to be polite by waiting in line, are left behind. The stereotypes of Greeks being pushy and rude are a result of these different attitudes towards space. This applies particularly to public space, which is taken just as the word implies – it's public – and therefore all are entitled to it, no matter who was there first. A useful phrase if someone jumps the line is *"será mou ínai tóra"* (it's my turn now).

Courtesy

You may feel that Greeks are not very courteous. They push in front of lines, drive aggressively, and don't give way on the sidewalk. This may be one of the most difficult and annoying aspects of living in Greece. Having said that, Greeks are wonderfully generous and warm once you get to know them, in which case their own politeness rules kick in. This politeness is based on solidarity, expressed by touching, use of diminutives in requests (*tha íthela ligáki neró parakaló* - "I'd like a little bit of water, please," but hoping for a full glass.), and formality (use of the plural) with older people and strangers.

Privacy

In Greece, people are constantly interacting with one another, and this is the preferred state of affairs. In the provinces, a Greek home is frequently bustling with neighbors and children popping in at will. The doors are open and no appointment needs to be made. There seems to be little opportunity for peace and quiet. "Time alone " is not generally valued by Greeks. Your neighbors may not understand if you want to be alone sometimes, and when you're alone they'll often come by to visit assuming you want company. This is not busybody or interfering behavior; it's a genuine concern for your well being. It's no wonder that the word for privacy does not translate directly into Greek. The concept doesn't exist. The closest terms are *monoxía*, which means loneliness (obviously with different connotations) or *isichía*, meaning peace.

The Bureaucracy

Dealing with bureaucracy will not only be irritating but time consuming. It is best to plan for the worst and allow plenty of time to get things taken care of, often all day with return trips. Information on what you need, say for an extension on your tourist visa, isn't easy to get, and the list of documents you need may change with each trip to the office.

Connections

Most Greeks have a *méson*, someone within the bureaucracy to pull strings for them or to help them through the bureaucratic maze (see *méson* on page 47). It helps when dealing with a particularly sticky bureaucratic issue to know someone in the office, or perhaps to get an influential Greek to help you out.

If you should need a lawyer, doctor, mover, or whatever, don't bother with the yellow pages - ask your friends. You will often be assured of much better service if you have an introduction to the professional you'll be dealing with.

Rules and Regulations

Disregarding rules and regulations is a national sport with little negative stigma attached to it. Outwitting authority by finding a loophole around the rules is often a source of pride. There is an expression in Greek, *"Tha to paráso ap'to paráthiro"* (I'll go through a window). The prevailing mentality seems to be that "these rules don't apply to me." The rules aren't always enforced either. There may be a flurry of enforcement, say for motorcyclists wearing helmets, but everyone knows the effort will be short-lived.

The Evil Eye *(to máti)*

Many Greeks, particularly those of the older generation and in rural areas, still believe in the evil eye. In can sometimes be cast unwittingly, especially by people with blue eyes. People who are envious are also prone to giving the evil eye, so you need to be careful when complimenting people, particularly children. If you are careless and forget and you see fear pass across a mother's face, you must say *"Panayía mazí tou"* (May the Virgin Mother be with him), make the sign of the cross and spit three times by saying "ptu, ptu, ptu" to remove any evil spell you may have cast. There are some women who are skilled at exorcising the evil eye, and in serious cases the priest may be called in. The talisman that protects against the evil eye is a small blue plastic eye, often rimmed in gold or silver, and worn on a chain around the neck, or pinned to the clothing for babies.

My adult students in Athens told me they weren't superstitious, but when I asked if they believed in the evil eye, they replied in unison: "well that's not a superstition, that's true."

Hospitality *(filoxénia)*

Greeks are traditionally very hospitable people and take great care in extending hospitality to their guests. Hospitality *(filoxénia*, which means "love of strangers") has been a custom in Greece since ancient times when it was believed any stranger might be Zeus in disguise so hospitality must be extended to him. Naturally, hospitality was more open handed before mass tourism. Nevertheless, especially in the less touristy areas, one may still experience the warmth and conviviality of Greek hospitality.

There is a whole ritual revolving around hospitality. When you visit a Greek home you will be offered, at the very least, something to drink. Should you refuse, your hostess may insist until you accept. Usually a Greek coffee, a glass of water, and a sweet are served, set out nicely on a tray with a doily. You may be served in the kitchen or in the "saloni," the living room, reserved for just this purpose. As you take the coffee say: *"Stín iyiá sas!"* – "Cheers!" If you are eating dinner in a Greek home the meal will be punctuated with pleas of *"Fi!"* (Eat). It is a good idea not to have eaten for several hours before going to a Greek home for dinner. It is polite to bring a small gift, usually some pastries, flowers, or a bottle of wine.

Smoking

Greeks are avid smokers and most public places are smoky. There are new rules stating that restaurants have "no smoking" sections, so if smoke bothers you, be sure to ask for them, although this will not apply to eating outdoors. Most ferry boats and trains have both smoking and non-smoking sections. Planes, buses, and public transportation are smoke free.

Greek Cultural Terms

The following are Greek cultural terms that don't have direct translations into English. Terms like these can give us insight into a culture.

Filótimo essentially means "love of honor", but this doesn't do the word justice. Even Greeks have difficulty describing the word, because it's an inexpressible aspect of self-esteem. It is a responsibility that is expressed by fulfilling obligations to the family, and it dictates proper behavior towards the family and others. A person's self-worth rests on

45

their *filótimo*. It is extremely important that a person's *filótimo* be upheld and respected by others. An important aspect of *filótimo* is that it depends on the judgment of the community, both friends and enemies. Essentially, if the community does not grant honor, then there is no honor, and an affront to *filótimo* (it can be "wounded") may have repercussions.

Paréa refers to the group of close friends who socialize together. Greeks translate it into English as "company" (of friends). *Paréas* will go out together, travel together, and have the habitual cup of coffee together. Some *paréas* last a lifetime. If you are out with a *paréa*, it's important to stay with them for the evening and not go home until everyone in the group does.

Kéfi is the sense of well-being and high spirits that is epitomized by Kazantzakis' Zorba. Spontaneous and exuberant, it is attained by being with your *paréa* and having just enough wine to drink so that life seems wonderful. On a typical evening out, everyone shares in the plates of food. Wineglasses are clinked to the toast of *"yámas"* ("to our health"). The idea is to loosen up and enjoy the food and friendship; however, getting drunk is frowned upon. If the spirit of *kéfi* is just right and Greek music is playing, your Greek friends will not be able to resist the urge to dance. The dance can be a sexy *tsiftéli* or a solemn *zeibékiko* (see *Dances* on page 74) and will be accompanied by clapping and shouts of *"ópa!"* Sometimes people dance on tables. In the past plates were broken, but this is now illegal.

Variéme is in a way the opposite of *kéfi*. It is related to boredom, or without *kéfi* at a particular time. When one is *variéme* it is a reason for not doing things, because in that mood, you wouldn't be able to do a good job.

Kérasma is treating someone to a coffee, drink, or meal. *Kérasma* is reciprocated on another occasion out, so that there is constant treating of one's friends. Note that Greeks never divvy up the bill according to who had what, although a bill may be split equally.

Meráki comes from a Turkish word, and means to do something, such as prepare a meal or make something, with care and passion.

Poniría translates roughly as wily or cunning, as in the "wily Odysseus." Greeks also use cunning and guile, *poniría*, in their competitive relations. It can be considered fair game to outsmart others in any kind of market dealings.

Koumbáros (m), *Koumbára* (f) is the term that applies to either the godparent or the bestman or maid of honor at a wedding. It is considered a spiritual kinship and establishes ties between unrelated families. For example, godparents would look after the welfare of the godchildren in the event of the death of the parents. Canon law forbids marriage between godchildren sharing the same godparent.

Pallikári is a young unmarried man with connotations of strength and bravery. It usually refers to the period after military service is completed and before marriage.

Levendi is a person who has dignity, with a heroic heart and a pure and noble soul.

Méson is a person with influence in the bureaucracy who pulls strings to get things done for you, such as completing papers or seeking medical care, or helping you get a good job.

Kamáki is a well known term in the tourist areas of Greece. It translates as "fishing harpoon" and refers to a Greek man who goes after foreign women with the intention of having sex, usually on a serial basis. Stereotypes about the ease in which tourist women are "conquered" are based on the women's nationality, so the first thing a *kamaki* will ask a foreign woman is where she's from.

To mesiméri is the siesta time after lunch that lasts until 5 p.m. or so. Calls shouldn't be made during this time. If you live near others, you should be quiet and respectful by not playing loud music. Businesses in the provinces may close during *to mesiméri*, but this practice was done away with in Athens because of the severe traffic problems caused by two commutes.

Vólta means 'a walk.' Especially on Sunday evenings, most squares *(platía)* and beachfronts *(paralía)* in summer are filled with strollers out for their *vólta*, to see and to be seen.

Kombolói are worry beads, made from amber, silver, gold, or plain glass, that are carried in the hand and clicked to relieve stress or pass the time.

47

Country Facts
History

The history of Greece is long and varied, and although Greece may lie geographically in Europe, her cultural heritage is more Eastern in nature. While Ancient Greece has influenced the West in countless ways, its influence was lost locally during the thousand years when Greece was part of the Byzantine Empire (330 – 1453 a.d.) and its four centuries under the Ottoman Turks (1453 – 1821). What's more, Greece didn't experience a Renaissance as northern Europe did.

The English name *Greece* comes from the Latin *Graecia*. The Greeks call themselves *Hellenes* and their country *Hellas* (*Elládha*). When the Modern Greek state was created in 1831, there were differences of opinion about the naming of the new state. The Byzantine Empire was decended from the Roman Empire and the population considered themselves *Romios*, not 'Greeks' or *Hellenes*. The notion of Hellenism had been renounced by the Orthodox Church during the Byzantine period because it was pagan and polytheistic. Nevertheless, the idea of claiming the heritage of the independent peoples of Classical Greece became central to the Greek independence movement, and this became compatible with identification with Byzantium. The Greek people were heirs to Hellas, but it was their adherence to the Orthodox faith that had kept their "Greek" identity alive during the Moslem Ottoman Empire period.

Modern Greeks now identify with both their Hellenistic past and the Byzantine Orthodox Church, and their culture retains traits of both Western rationalism and Oriental mysticism.

This section on history is intended as an outline of some of the main historical points. The dates used for each period are approximate and are meant only to set a chronological framework.

A Brief Outline of Greek History

6000 – 4000 B.C.	Neolithic Period (page 49)
2800 – 1500 B.C.	Minoan Period (page 49)
1500 – 1100 B.C.	Mycenean Period (page 51)
1100 – 800 B.C.	"Dark Ages" (page 53)
800 – 500 B.C.	Archaic Period (page 53)
500 – 400 B.C.	Classical Period (page 56)
400 – 200 B.C.	Hellenistic Period (page 57)
200 B.C. – 330 A.D.	Roman Period (page 58)
330 A.D. – 1453 A.D.	Byzantine Period (page 59)
1453 – 1821 A.D.	Ottoman Period (page 61)
1821 – 1829 A.D.	War of Independence (page 61)
1831 – Present	Modern Greek Period (page 62)

Neolithic Period 6000 – 4000 B.C.

There are Neolithic sites scattered around Greece; the best preserved are in Thessaly near Volos. The settlements were small hunting and gathering and farming communities. They worshipped clay fertility goddesses, worked obsidian to make tools, and made pottery.

Minoan Period 2800 – 1500 B.C.

The Minoans were a sea trading civilization. They built grand palaces on Crete which were centers of peaceful and sophisticated life. We know they were peaceful because they were built without defenses. The most important palaces were at Knossos and Festos. The walls of the palaces were decorated with delightful frescos depicting scenes from nature; today these reconstructed frescos can be seen in the museum in Iraklion, Crete. The Minoans revered bulls, which are pictured in many of these murals, on jewelry, and in the famous legend of Theseus. The Minoan Period is also called The Bronze Age; technologically, bronze was the main metal in wide use for tools.

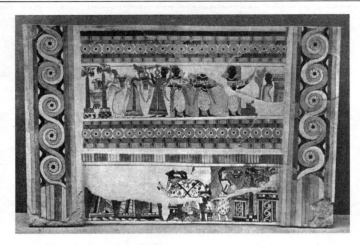

The legend of Theseus is the main surviving myth of this period. Theseus was the son of Aegeus, king of Athens. Athens and Crete had a treaty by which seven boys and seven girls were sent annually to Crete as tribute to be devoured by the half-man, half-bull Minotaur, who lived in the labyrinth at Knossos. Theseus volunteered to go to Crete as one of the victims. Before Theseus left Athens, his father had asked that when their ship returned they should fly a white sail if Theseus had survived and a black one if he had not. When he reached Knossos, Ariadne, the daughter of King Minos, fell in love with him and gave him a thread so he could find his way back out of the labyrinth. Theseus found his way to the heart of the labyrinth and killed the Minotaur. Then he used his thread to escape. Ariadne and Theseus fled the island together, ending up on Naxos; there he abandoned her. Theseus, returning to Athens alone, forgot to fly the white sail. King Aegeus, seeing the black sail from the shore, plunged into the sea in despair. The Aegean Sea is named after him. Crafty Theseus became king.

Around 1450 B.C., the Minoan civilization was weakened by a volcanic eruption on the island of Santorini, a Minoan outpost. Some scholars believe that Santorini is the original of the legendary lost island of Atlantis. About a century later the palaces on Crete were sacked and burned, probably by the Myceneans from the Peloponnese on the Greek mainland. Minoan writing was preserved on clay tablets that were fired in the cataclysm. Their script is called Linear A by archaeologists and has not yet been deciphered. It appears to be neither Greek nor any other Indo-European language; some scholars think it may be a Semitic language.

50

Mycenean Period 1500 – 1100 B.C.

This period is named after the citadel at Mycenae in the Peloponnese. The Myceneans were more war-like than the Minoans, as evidenced by the many bronze weapons they left behind and their massive fortifications. Early in their history these Myceneans had had important contact with the Minoans. They had even adopted a similar script, called by archaeologists Linear B, to write the Mycenean language. Linear B has been deciphered, and the language is a proto-Greek.

The Lion Gate at Mycenae

The Homeric legends are from this Mycenean Period. They were preserved by oral tradition for 400 years until in the eighth century b.c. the poet Homer set them down in *The Iliad* and *The Odyssey*. These epic poems, widely accepted as being among the greatest works of human literature, tell the story of the Trojan War. Long dismissed as works of fiction, they were believed to be history by the ancient Greeks and are now widely accepted as history by modern historians and archeologists – not the details, but the main story. As we now interpret that story (based on discoveries since 2000), around 1250 B.C. the Mycenean Greeks fought the Trojans, who were a Semitic people. Their capital, Troy, was a city which was vassal to the Hittites, a great Semitic kingdom that ruled most of Asia Minor, what is now Turkey. Because of its position, Troy controlled the straits connecting the Mediterranean and Black Seas, and it had become very wealthy. The Trojans called their city *Ilium* or, in Hittite, *Wilusiya*; the name Troy comes from the region they ruled, *Troia*. Today you can visit the site of Troy at *Hissarlik* in Turkey where archeologist Manfred Korfmann is directing the excavations and making new and exciting finds.

In *The Iliad*, Helen, wife of Menelaus, king of Sparta, had been taken to Troy by the Trojan prince, Paris. Menelaus and his brother, King Agamemnon of Mycenae, gathered 1200 ships and men from all over Greece to wage war against the Trojans. Among the leaders were Nestor of Pylos, Odysseus from the nearby Ionian island of Ithaca, and Achilles from central Greece. Then there was a problem. The fleet was rigged and ready to sail, but the winds would not blow. Agamemnon had

51

offended Artemis, the goddess of the hunt, by killing one of her favorite stags. She would only be appeased by the sacrifice of Iphigenia, daughter of Agamemnon and Clytemnestra. After the sacrifice, the winds came up and the ships set sail for the siege against Troy. The king was pleased, but Clytemnestra spent the ensuing years plotting her revenge against Agamemnon for sacrificing their daughter.

Menelaus.　　Paris.　　Diomedes.　　Odysseus.　　Nestor.　　Achilles.　　Agamemnon.

The Iliad describes the events of the ten-year Trojan War. The main action happens towards the end of the war; Achilles, the greatest Greek hero, takes revenge on Hector, the greatest Trojan hero, for having killed his beloved friend Patroclus. The end of the story is told in *The Odyssey*. First, Achilles is assassinated by Paris during peace negotiations. With the Trojan and Greek champions both dead, the fighting and intrigue continued until the Greeks led by wily Odysseus finally took Troy by the famous subterfuge of the Trojan horse. The Trojan princess Cassandra had warned her countrymen to "beware of Greeks bearing gifts," but her pleas had fallen on deaf ears. She had been given the gift of prophecy by the god Apollo who had loved her, but when she rejected him, he amended his gift saying that no one would believe her when she told the truth. After Troy fell, Agamemnon took Cassandra as his captured slave and concubine and returned to Mycenae. All during the war Clytemnestra, Agamemnon's queen, had waited for this moment. She had sentries on the alert to send back news of the end of the war. As soon as Agamemnon and Cassandra arrived home, Clytemnestra slew him "like an ox in the manger." The rest of *The Odyssey* tells the wonderful story of Odysseus' journey and adventures as he took another ten long years to return home to Ithaca, his island.

In the mid-19th century, the romantic adventurer Heinrich Schliemann discovered and excavated both Mycenae and Troy – with a shovel in

Schliemann's Myceanan mask of "Agamemnon"

one hand and a copy of Homer in the other. Many magnificent treasures come from this period of discovery. The Myceanean finds are on display in the National Museum in Athens. The main Hittite find from Troy was the so-called Treasure of Priam, King of Troy. Schliemann left this hoard of precious jewelry and gold to the Berlin museum where after World War II it went missing; it resurfaced in 1994 in St. Petersburg, Russia. Many of Homer's details may have been taken from other Myceanean legends and added to the story of Troy, but today most archeologists accept Schliemann's find at *Hissarlik* as the true site of the Trojan War.

"Dark Ages" 1100 – 800 B.C.

In the 12th century B.C., the Dorians, barbarians from the north, invaded Greece. This caused a shift of populations as the original Greek inhabitants spread out into the area around the Black Sea and the coast of Asia Minor. The glorious Mycenean period was shattered, and Greece fell into serious decline. The great Mycenean palaces fell into ruin and were never rebuilt. Remaining settlements were small and poor, populated by farmers and artisans. The art of writing disappeared and trade dwindled. However, even during this dark three-hundred-year period, there were both material innovations such as geometric pottery and technological advances like the emergence of iron for use in tools, weapons, and small objects.

Archaic Period 800 – 500 B.C.

This period saw the rise of the *pólis*, autonomous city-states. These were ruled by tyrants, usurpers of power, some of whom were benevolent and others evil. Ionian Athens and Dorian Sparta in the Peloponnese were the two most powerful city-states. Sparta was austere and militaristic while Athens was more sophisticated and aesthetic. Then at the beginning of the sixth century (594 B.C.), Solon was elected leader and he introduced sweeping reforms which paved the way for the emergence of Athenian democracy in the next century. He also encouraged his countrymen to plant olive trees, still a staple of the Greek diet today.

The Archaic Period was an era of great accomplishments. Architecturally, temples in the Doric style were built to house statues of deities. Artistic development flourished with monumental stone sculptures in the 'Archaic style,' which is characterized by the slight motion of one foot in front of the other and the so-called "Archaic smile". Innovations were made in ceramics; black figures, depicting daily life or the gods, were painted on red pottery. Toward the end of the sixth century B.C., this style developed into the more sophisticated and graceful red figure pottery.

A Late Archaic
black figure vase

A horseman with
the Archaic smile

Coinage was invented and put into use as a means of exchange. The Greek alphabet first appeared; it was based on the Phoenician original and was the forerunner of our own. Homer wrote during this period, as did Hesiod, Aesop, and lyric poets such as Sappho of Lesbos. There were early experiments in the art of theater, based on the worship of Dionysus. Ionia in Asia Minor saw the beginning of scientific inquiry and philosophical thought, and Pythagoras began investigating geometry and its relationship to music. And this was also the period when the Olympic Games began in Olympia in 776.

Twelve gods were predominant in the religion of the Greeks from the Archaic Period on. Each god had his or her own area of expertise. Some were associated with natural realms like the sun or the sea, and although they were all thought to reside on Mt. Olympus, many were also associated with various places around Greece. Two other gods, one of wine and the other of grain, joined the pantheon later. Detailed information on all the Greek gods, heroes, and myths is available at www.mythome.org/greek.html and at www.mythweb.com. The Roman names for these twelve Olympians are given in parentheses on page 55.

The Twelve Olympians

Athena   **Artemis**

Zeus *(Jupiter)* – Olympia and Athens, brother of Poseidon and Hades, leader and father of the gods, lightning and thunder

Hera *(Juno)* – Zeus's long suffering wife and sister, the goddess of marriage and childbirth

Poseidon *(Neptune)* – Argos, Isthmia, god of the sea, earthquakes, and horses

Hades (Pluto) – brother of Zeus and Poseidon, god of the dead and the underworld, of the mineral wealth from the earth

Athena *(Minerva)* – Athens, daughter and favorite of Zeus, goddess of wisdom, the owl is her symbol

Apollo *(Apollo)* – Delphi, god of the sun and of music and healing

Artemis *(Diana)* – Arcadia, goddess of the moon, of chastity, and of the hunt, Apollo's twin and Zeus's daughter

Aphrodite *(Venus)* – Corinth, goddess of desire, love, and beauty

Hestia *(Vesta)* – Goddess of the hearth and home

Ares *(Mars)* – Thrace and Sparta, son of Zeus, god of war

Hermes *(Mercury)* – Arcadia, son of Zeus, messenger of the gods, god of travelers, merchants, and thieves; invented the lyre

Iphestos [Hephaestus] *(Vulcan)* – Ephesus and Mt. Aetna, god of fire and the forge (blacksmiths, weavers) and of volcanos

Two later Olympians with important cults

Dionysus *(Bacchus)* – Thrace and Phrygia, god of wine and fertility, of artistic inspiration and destructive rage

Demeter *(Ceres)* – Ellipsis, goddess of the earth and of agriculture

Before the Olympians, their parents, the Titans or elder gods, included Gaea (the earth mother), Uranus (the sky god), Cronus (Uranus's son who killed him and became king and then was killed by his own son, Zeus), Hyperion (the sun), Phoebe (the moon), Oceanus (the seas), and Prometheus(gave fire to man and sided with and betrayed by Zeus).

Classical Period 500 – 400 B.C.

In 490 B.C. the Persians, intent on expanding their empire, attacked the Athenian territory at Marathon. The Athenians won the Battle of Marathon, but the Persian siege lasted another ten years until the Athenians' decisive naval victory at Salamis. According to the historian Herodotus, the Persians lost because of their excessive pride, *hubris*, while the Athenians were victorious because of the favor and protection of the Greek gods.

The Acropolis of Pericles

As is well-known, during the Classical Period, Athens became the birthplace of democracy, which thrived under the administration of the visionary and incorruptible Pericles (495-429 B.C.). Under his leadership, art, literature, science, and philosophy flourished. The Parthenon, a temple to Athena, constructed in both Doric style and the newer and more graceful Ionic style, was built on the Acropolis. Socrates (469-399 B.C.) was the great philosopher of the age. Some of the most profound and inventive drama ever written was created in this era. Aristophanes wrote comedies, and Aeschylus, Sophocles, and Euripides, tragedies. Their plays were performed in the theaters of Athens, Epidauros, and elsewhere.

In this glorious Classical Period, a view of humankind became widely accepted that one should live in moderation, cultivating a proper balance and order in one's life. Humans were understood to be free yet flawed, so undue pride, *hubris*, was a human failing punishable by the gods. The quest to establish order out of chaos was the aim of civic endeavor and artistic and philosophical expression.

With cultural dominance, Athens grew in wealth and political power, and naturally it expanded the alliance of *pólis* toward Sparta, that very different *pólis*, dedicated to civic conformity, austerity, and militarism. Eventually war erupted. The Peloponnesian War (431-404 B.C.), chronicled by Thucydides, lasted nearly thirty years and ended in the defeat of Athens. During this time a plague broke out in Athens, and Pericles died. The inevitable devastation of war and the death of Pericles demoralized the Athenians and their allies, marked the end the "golden" Classical Period, and led to the decline of democracy and the independent *pólis* in Greece.

Hellenistic Period 400 – 200 B.C.

Socrates was condemned to death in 399 B.C. The charge was corrupting the minds of the youth and disagreeing with the idea that the state had the right to dictate the opinions of the individual. Socrates' student, Plato (427-347 B.C.), became disenchanted with civic life and the reality of democracy; in response he wrote *The Republic* on the nature of justice. Plato also opened the Academy, a research institute, whose most famous pupil was Aristotle (384-322 B.C.), the originator of the scientific method of inquiry. Aristotle in turn became the tutor of Alexander the Great (356-323 B.C.).

In 336 B.C., Alexander, at the age of twenty, inherited Macedonia, an undeveloped, militaristic kingdom in the north of Greece, and his father's army. Following his father's plan, he swiftly completed and consolidated the conquest of the rest of Greece and then, leading the Greek army, invaded and took Asia Minor from the Persian empire. Perhaps because of his rapid success, suddenly he had a new ambition, to conquer the world and spread Greek civilization worldwide. Without hesitation, he led his army around the Mediterranean to seize Egypt. There he started a new capital, Alexandria. Then he expanded his empire into the East through Persia and Afghanistan and into India. He had conquered the "known" world between 336 and 323 B.C. During this short period, a new world order was created; along with Alexander's military control came the Greek (Hellenic) culture and language. For more information on Alexander, visit www.1stmuse.com/frames.

When Alexander died at the age of 33 in 323 B.C., his empire split into three separate Hellenistic dynasties, the most important being the Ptolemies in Egypt. They created the greatest library in the world in Alexandria, and under their patronage advances were made in the scientific fields of medicine, astronomy, and mathematics. Nearly 300 years later, the last and most famous ruler of the Ptolemies was Queen Cleopatra (69-30 B.C.).

Meanwhile, back in Athens three new philosophical schools had developed: the Cynics, Epicureans and Stoics. These grew out of disenchantment with the old order and a new focus on individualism. The visual arts continued to flourish and change. Sculptures of gods, women, and men had more sense of movement; they were more dramatic and sensuous, more realistic and mannered. The Venus de Milo is from this period. Artistic innovations also included mosaics and blown glass. Architecturally the Corinthian style, more ornate than the earlier Doric and Ionic styles, became fashionable especially in the interiors of temples.

The Roman Period 200 B.C. – 330 A.D.

During the era of the Roman Republic (500 – 27 B.C.), the Romans had taken the Hellenistic colonies on the Italian peninsula and in Sicily. Beginning their long drive to empire, the Romans began their campaign into Greece in 215 B.C. As Rome and Greece traded and then fought over territory, the Romans won political control but fell increasingly under the influence of Greek culture. Roman art, literature, religion, and philosophy became more Greek while Greece proper gradually fell into decline and became a provincial backwater state of the Roman Empire. Then during the early Roman Empire (27 B.C. – 292 A.D.), although Greece remained economically and politically unimportant, Greek businessmen and civil servants working for the Emperors developed great personal wealth and political influence. One of the few institutions which remained vital in Greece was the ancient Olympic Games which became a favorite Roman imperial tradition. The Emperor Nero so loved the Olympics that he participated personally in 69 A.D. He drove in a chariot race and "won," although he fell out of his chariot and didn't finish the race.

The city of Byzantium was added to the Macedonian kingdom in 340 B.C. by Philip, Alexander's father, and during the Hellenistic and Roman Periods, it slowly gained in prosperity and influence. Because of its importance, the Romans had one of their vital Roman military roads, the Via Egnatia, built in 146 B.C. connecting Rome and Byzantium. It was maintained and expanded under the Empire.

Byzantium 330 – 1453 A.D.

Constantine (c. 274-337 A.D.) defeated his rivals and became Emperor in 324 A.D. During the final battle, he saw a miraculous image in the sky and heard the voice say, "In this sign conquer." It was both a symbol of Zoroastrianism, a favorite religion in his army, and a Christian cross. When he won, he pleased his mother, Helen, by making Christianity the official religion of his empire, but he allowed the other religions and cults popular in the empire to survive. In 330 A.D., he officially moved his government to the most important Greek city, Byzantium. He then changed its name to Constantinople, and declared it "the new Rome," his Christian capital. Symbolically, Greece had finally overcome the influence of Italy in the Empire. In 476, the last Western Roman Emperor was overthrown and replaced by the German barbarian king Odoacer, and the city was sacked by the barbarians and rebelling slaves.

Haggia Sophia
begun in 534 A.D.
by Emperor Justinian

Rome survived 476 and the Pope in Rome remained the symbolic head of the Christian church, but both were diminished in power. By contrast, in the East the now independent Byzantine Empire and its Greek capital, Constantinople, prospered both as a military, commercial power and as the center of spreading, flourishing Christianity. The western Holy Roman Empire slowly declined into the Dark Ages, and Constantinople was clearly the heir and capital of European civilization.

The Christian church remained formally united until in 1054 a rift developed, the Great Schism. Christianity split into the Eastern (Orthodox) and the Roman (Catholic) churches. The disagreement was over the infallibility of the Pope and the wording of the Nicene Creed. The Orthodox Church states that the Holy Spirit proceeds from God the Father. The Catholic Church contends it proceeds from both the Father and the Son.

The walls of Constantinople as they were in 1204 when the Greek city fell to the Venetians and Franks of the Fourth Crusade

Photographed after a 20th Century restoration

In 1204 the German (Frankish) and Latin knights of the Fourth Crusade were on their way to capture Moslem Jerusalem in the Holy Land for the Roman Catholic Church. The Venetians, who were transporting them, plotted with some of the Crusade leaders to stop first in Constantinople, capture it, and reunite Christendom under the Pope. In the process, the Crusaders sacked and burned Constantinople, plundering the accumulated wealth of a thousand years, and then put a Latin emperor on the Byzantine throne. In fact, the Crusaders had so much loot that they gave up going to Jerusalem and sailed home.

Sultan Mehmed leads the Ottoman army into fallen Constantinople/Istanbul in 1453

Following this misguided crusade, assorted "Franks" led by the ever acquisitive Venetians moved into the rest of Greece, especially the islands, and set up a feudal system, imposing the supremacy of the Roman Catholic Church and putting themselves in charge of trade. (There are still Roman Catholics living in Greece to this day, descendants of the original Venetians.) Byzantine Constantinople under its Latin Emperor never quite recovered from the sacking of the Fourth Crusade. It slowly declined in influence, and in 1453 it fell to the Muslim Ottoman Turks.

Over the next few centuries, Greece was divided and torn by a power struggle between the Venetians in the islands and the Turks in the capital, the Greek mainland, and Anatolia. The Greeks were essentially caught in the middle, living as vulnerable pawns between the two powers.

Ottoman Period 1453 – 1821

The Turks considered the Greeks to be a distinct ethnic group and allowed them to keep their religion. Adherence to the Orthodox faith during the Turkish occupation kept Greek identity alive. However, the Ottoman rule of Greece was hard, characterized by taxes and serfdom. Greatly feared by the Greeks was the "child levy" that was paid every few years wen they were forced to send their healthy boys to serve in the Sultan's Moslem Janissary army.

As it had been in the Byzantine Period, rural Greece was agricultural and the center of life was the village. Day-to-day Ottoman rule was characterized by both corruption and indifference on the part of local officials. Because of this negligence, lawlessness flourished; pirates prowled the sea and *kléfts* (bandits) held sway in the mountains. However, in Constantinople and Smyrna (Izmir), Greek merchants and educated professionals prospered; Greeks often held high positions in the Ottoman administration. In the late 15th century, Sephardic Jews, who had suffered under the Spanish Inquisition, made their way into the Ottoman Empire at the invitation of the Sultan. A large Jewish population flourished in Thessaloniki until World War II.

In the on-going power struggle between the Venetians and the Turks, the Venetians waged an attack on Athens in the late 17th century. A mortar hit the Parthenon, where Turkish gunpowder was stored, causing the damage that you see today.

The **War for Independence** began in 1821 when *kléfts*, Greek brigands hiding in the mountains, began to revolt. This Robin Hood-style revolt captured the imaginations of many Greeks and Western Europeans. European "philhellenes" got into the act, sending money and men. The most famous was the romantic poet Lord Byron, who died in Greece in 1824. The struggle for independence lasted until 1829.

Led by **kléft** *fighter Teodoros Kolokotronis (1770-1834), Greek revolutionary forces defeated the Turkish army at Dramatis in 1822.*

61

Modern Greece 1831 – present

In 1831 the Modern Greek state was established. Borders were drawn and a "Greek" monarchy was contrived by European powers; a Bavarian prince became King Otto I of Greece. The state at that time was made up of the Peloponnese, central Greece, and the Cyclades. Only 800,000 of the six million Greeks living in the Ottoman Empire lived in this original territory, but the government's policy was to bring all the Greek populations under Greek rule. Thessaly became part of Greece in 1881. In 1910 the great statesman Eleftherios Venizelos became Prime Minister. He reenergized the consolidation movement, and after bitter struggles in the Balkan Wars (1912-13), parts of Epirus, Macedonia, Thrace, Crete, and some islands close to modern day Turkey became part of Greece in 1913.

The complexity and difficulties of Greek history and social experience in the 20th century, and its impact on Greek society and Greek mindset, cannot be over emphasized. The following is meant only as a very brief and superficial outline of events. In order to further delve into the complexity and the consequences of these events, please take a look at some of the books in the bibliography.

Eleftherios Venizelos

The foreign policy at the time of World War I, called the Great Idea (*Megáli Idhéa*), was to liberate the Greek populations still under Ottoman domain. The ill-conceived Anatolian campaign in 1922 to liberate Smyrna (Izmir) failed miserably (*To katastrofí*). The Turks led by the founder of modern Turkey, Kemal Mustafa (Ataturk) roundly defeated the Greeks as they marched towards Ankara.

The result of this campaign was the 1923 Treaty of Lausanne. In a great population exchange of 1,300,000 people, all surviving Christians in Asia Minor were relocated to Greece. Many of these refugees were sophisticated and well educated, yet arrived in their new homeland destitute with just what they could carry; many of them spoke only Turkish. Most Muslims in the new Greek state went to Turkey, with the exception of a few who remained in Thrace. This caused great and enduring bitterness in Greece.

As was true in much of Europe, the period between the world wars was one of constant political unrest and confusion. Monarchs were overthrown. A republic begun in 1924 was succeeded by a rightist dictatorship in 1936.

During World War II, Greece was occupied by both the Italians and the Germans *(see the explanation of* Ochi Day, *page 38)*. There was mass starvation; entire villages were destroyed and in some cases their inhabitants executed. Following the war, Greece experienced a devastating civil war between communists and monarchists; thousands were killed, and many Communists *(andártes)* fled to Eastern Europe. The Communist Party in Greece was banned for the next 25 years. Reconstruction began under the Truman Doctrine in 1947. American policy in Greece was one of containment, to prevent Communism from spreading to the southern tip of the Balkans. The monarchy was restored, and twenty years of relative peace, prosperity, and political instability followed.

On April 21, 1967, tanks rolled into Athens, and a military dictatorship, led by Col. Papadopoulos, seized power. King Constantine left the country after a failed counter-coup some months later. Many people in Greece believed that the CIA had organized the "putsch." Without question, the junta was anti-Communist and so was supported by the Johnson and Nixon administrations (for which President Clinton apologized to the Greek people in 1999). Under the dictatorship, human rights were disregarded, and those who spoke out against the Colonels were jailed and often tortured. Newspapers were censored, the music of Theodorakis and others was banned, and many prominent Greeks went into exile. On November 17, 1973, the students of the Polytechnio University in Athens reacted to the repression of the regime and barricaded themselves inside their school. The army sent in tanks leaving many dead and wounded. In 1974 the Colonels attempted to take over Cyprus, provoking a Turkish invasion of the island. After a mutiny within the ranks of the colonels, the junta collapsed.

After the fall of the junta, democracy was immediately restored. The Greek statesman Constantine Karamanlis returned from exile to become prime minister. The Colonels were tried for treason and sent to prison for life. Greece became a full member of the European Union in 1981.

Today the two main parties are the conservative party, *Nea Dhimokratia*, and socialist *PASOK* (Panhellenic Socialic Movement). *PASOK*, founded and led by the populist Andreas Papandreau, held power from 1981 to 1989. During that time there were many reforms including laws that helped equalize the status of women and aid to farmers in the form of subsidies. There were also scandals which led to the election of Constatine Mitsotakis, of *Nea Dhimokratia*, who held power for a brief period between 1990 and

Andreas Papandreau
PASOK 1981-89, 1993-96

1993. *Nea Dhimokratia* was beset with double-digit inflation and unpopular austerity programs which led to the reelection of Papandreau and *PASOK* in 1993. Papandreau died in 1996 and Konstantinos Simitis, of *PASOK*, became prime minister.

Costas Karamanlis
Nea Dhimokratia 2004-

By 2004 severe economic problems, charges of corruption, and lagging preparations for the Summer Olympics, undermined the popularity of *PASOK*. Simitis tried to shift his party to the right, but the electorate wasn't convinced. *PASOK* lost the election to *Nea Dhimokratia* led by Costas Karamanlis. The new government is trying to salvage the Olympics and at the same time develop a more stable and peaceful relationship with Turkey.

The Land

Greece is in the southernmost portion of the Balkan Peninsula and covers 52,000 square miles. There are countless islands, some of them uninhabited. Greece is mountainous with nearly 40% of the country situated over 1500 feet.

Greece is divided into 13 administrative regions and 51 departments (see map, pp. 66-67). The administrative regions include Epirus, Macedonia, Thrace, and Thessaly to the north. Greece's second largest city is Thessaloniki in Macedonia (not to be confused with the independent country of Macedonia north of Greece). Athens is in the region known as Attica, and the peninsula south and west of Athens is known as the Peloponnese. The Ionian Islands are on the west coast of Greece, the Cycladese and Dodecanese Islands are in the Aegean Sea, east of the mainland, and the largest island, Crete, is to the south.

The People

The population of Greece is almost 11,000,000. 96% are ethnic Greeks. Throughout Greek history, there have been incursions into Greece by Dorians, Venetians, Turks, Slavs, Albanians, and others. Many of these groups have been assimilated as Greeks over the centuries.

The main minorities in Greece are Vlachs, Sarakatsani, Jews, and Turks. The Vlachs are traditionally migrant shepherds who live in the Pindus Mountains in northwestern Greece. Their language is related to Latin rather than Greek. Another group of shepherds are the Sarakatsani, who speak Greek. They were traditionally nomadic and traveled around the Balkan Peninsula and Anatolia.

There were two waves of Jewish settlers in Greece, the first during Classical times. The next wave were the Sephardim who had been ousted from Spain during the inquisition. They settled in several places in Greece, but their primary center was Thessaloniki. During World War II, 85% of Greek Jews were sent to concentration camps, where most of them perished. There are two excellent Jewish Museums, one in Athens and another one in Thessaloniki describing their history in Greece.

The Turkish Muslims live mostly in Thrace, in the northeast, bordering Turkey. About 100,000 Thracian Muslims were allowed to remain at the time of the population exchanges (see *History, Modern Greece* page 62).

The New Immigrants

The Albanians and Greeks have always had tense relations. In northwestern Greece, part of historic Epirus lies in Albania; thus there are Greeks living behind the Albanian border. Since Albania opened its borders in 1990, there has been an influx of impoverished Albanians entering Greece in search of work. They do hard day labor and are not usually paid the going rate. Some of them live in hovels in large groups, trying to save money to take back home. Many others are rapidly assimilating.

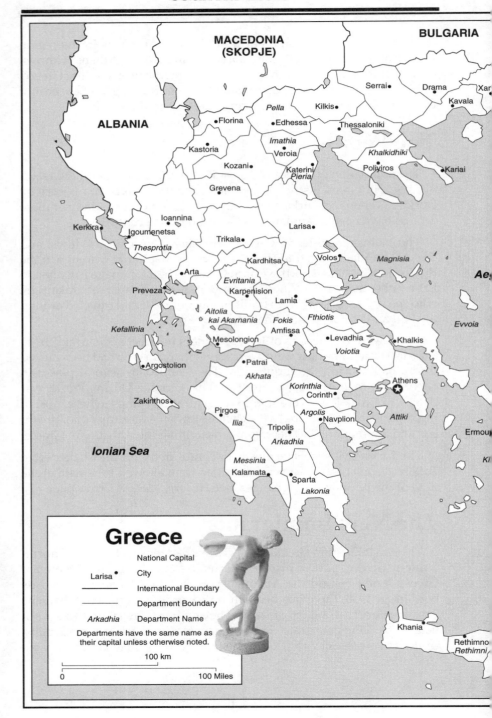

BULGARIA

MACEDONIA (SKOPJE)

ALBANIA

Serrai • Drama • Xar
Kavala
Pella Kilkis •
• Florina • Edhessa Thessaloniki
Imathia
Kastoria • Veroia Khalkidhiki
Kozani • Katerini Poliyiros • • Kariai
Pieria
Grevena •

Ioannina • Larisa •
Kerkira • Igoumenetsa
Thesprotia Trikala •
Kardhitsa • Volos Magnisia
• Arta Ae
Preveza • Evritania Karpenision
Lamia •
Aitolia Fokis Fthiotis
kai Akarnania Amfissa Evvoia
Kefallinia • Mesolongion • Levadhia • Khalkis
Voiotia
• Patrai
• Argostolion Akhata
Korinthia Athens
Zakinthos • Corinth •
Pirgos • Argolis Attiki
Ilia Navplion Ermou
Tripolis •
Arkadhia

Ionian Sea Messinia
Kalamata • • Sparta
Lakonia Ki

Greece

National Capital
Larisa • City
International Boundary
Department Boundary
Arkadhia Department Name
Departments have the same name as
their capital unless otherwise noted.

100 km
0 100 Miles

Khania •
Rethimno
Rethimni

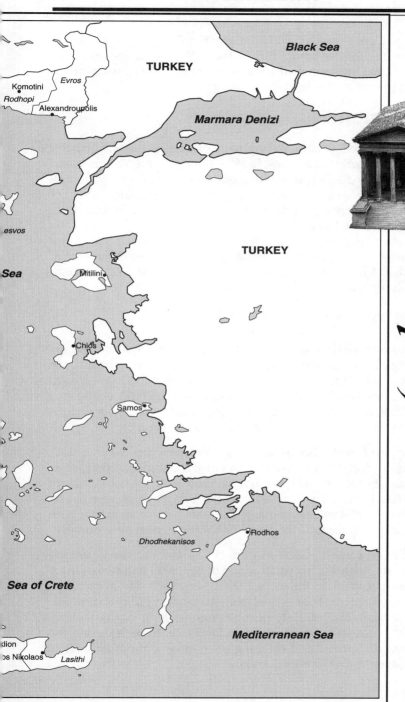

Black Sea

TURKEY

Komotini
Evros
Rodhopi
Alexandroupolis

Marmara Denizi

.esvos

Sea
Mitilini

TURKEY

Chios

Samos

Rodhos

Dhodhekanisos

Sea of Crete

Mediterranean Sea

klion
s Nikolaos
Lasithi

Map of Greece

Today there are about 800,000 immigrants in Greece (census 2001), people from the former Soviet Bloc, Asians, Kurds, Arabs, and Africans. Greece, having been a fairly homogenous country for centuries, is adapting to the new multi-cultural reality.

Government

The Modern Greek state was originally established as a monarchy by the northern European nations. In 1975, there was a referendum and the monarchy was discontinued. Greece is now a constitutional republic with a 300-member parliament (*voúli*). The prime minister is head of the government, and the president is the ceremonial head of state. Public officials are elected. It is required by law that all Greek adults vote. There are two main parties, the conservative *Nea Dhimokratia* party, and *PASOK* (Panhellenic Socialist Movement). There are also other smaller parties such as a few left-wing parties. Greece is a full and active member of the European Union (EU).

Economy

Agriculture employs one-third of the population. The main crops are olives, wine, grain, cotton, tobacco, and fresh fruits. Greece is one of the least industrialized members of the European Union with most businesses being small family-owned operations. In 1990, eighty-five percent of the industries in Greece employed fewer than ten people. Women play an active role in all spheres of the workplace.

Shipping is well established in Greece. Greek ship owners like Onassis or Niarchos were world renowned, not only for their accomplishments as shipping magnates, but also for their flamboyant lifestyles. In the not too distant past, many Greek men were attracted to working on the ships as an opportunity to see the world and earn a living. The many who seem to have been "captain" will gladly recite all the places they've been to on their journeys.

Mass tourism came to Greece in the 1960's and has been growing ever since. For instance, the small island of Santorini had two or three boat arrivals per week in the early 1970's. Now each day in the summer, it has several ferry boat arrivals and many direct flights from Europe. Cruise boats also call into port all summer long. Many farmers have built "rooms to let" on their farm land to earn cash during the summer season. Tourism and shipping are two very important means by which Greece earns foreign currency.

Besides agricultural products Greece exports cement, textiles, ore, and chemicals. It imports cars, electronic items, and other consumer goods, as well as food. Its imports exceed its exports, but this is offset somewhat by shipping, tourism, and remittances from Greek expatriates abroad.

Education

Because of the benefits offered to the well educated, education is highly valued in Greece. It is free and compulsory. The educational system has a primary school, grades 1-6; gymnasium (middle school), grades 7-9; and lyceum (high school), grades 10-12. There are two types of lyceum: technical-vocational and general.

Universities and polytechnics are also free, but admission policies limit the number of places available each year. The university entrance exams are rigorous and competitive; not all of those who wish to study are accepted to university. Many Greek students opt to study abroad; those who can afford it go to Western Europe or the U.S., and others go to former Soviet Bloc countries.

Private tutoring schools, *frontistíria*, exist all over Greece to help students prepare for exams and learn languages. English is only recently being taught in public schools, yet these courses are widely supplemented at *frontistíria*.

Literature

In the late 19th century in Greece, the literary movement called the New School of Athens was producing short stories and some novels. These were based on village life and some of the cultural changes taking place at that time. One of the main authors of this period was Alexandros Papadiamantis (1851-1911). An example of his works is *The Murderess*, which looks at the psyche of a village woman who in response to oppressive village life turns to violence. A wonderful book of Papadiamantis' short stories has been translated into English (see *Greek Literature in Translation* listed on page 91).

Nikos Kazantzakis (1883-1957) is the most well-known Greek author outside of Greece. His most famous book is *Zorba*, due in part to Anthony Quinn's excellent performance as the lusty lover of life who dances away his sorrows. His book *The Last Temptation of Christ* upset the Greek Orthodox Church, so he was not allowed to be buried in a church cemetery. His grave is on the old Venetian Wall in his hometown of Iraklion, Crete. The inscription on his gravestone sums up his beliefs: "I fear nothing, I hope for nothing, I am free."

Kedros Publishers in Athens has an excellent series of "Modern Greek Writers." It offers translations of such writers as Dido Sotiriou (*Farewell Anatolia*), Alki Zei (*Achilles' Fiancee*), and Maro Douka (*Fool's Gold*).

Poetry is an important literary form in Greece, which has had two Nobel laureates, George Seferis and Odysseus Elytis. George Seferis (1900-1971) was born in Asia Minor. He wrote in free verse about separation, nostalgia and loss. His poetry has been compared to that of T.S. Eliot. Odysseus Elytis (1911-1993), was born in Crete. He wrote about the search for a national identity and was more sympathetic to the mystical Eastern aspect of the Greek character than to its rational Western strain. He also writes about the force of sun and light in Greece.

Some of the main themes of Greek poetry are the search for national identity, the quest for freedom, classical myths, religious beliefs, and nature. Constantine Kavafis (1863-1933) is considered the forerunner of Modern Greek poetry. He was born in Alexandria, Egypt. One of his best-loved poems is "Ithaca," which describes Odysseus's voyage back to his homeland after the Trojan War. The main theme of the poem is that the voyage may be more important than what one finds at the end of the journey.

Yannis Ritsos, another well-known poet, was born in 1909 in the Peloponnese. He was imprisoned during the civil war and again during the junta because of his left-wing ideology. Ritsos wrote social protest, with humanitarian concern for those who suffer. He was nominated several times for the Nobel Prize and received the Lenin Prize in 1977. He died in 1990.

Theater

With about forty-five theaters, Athens has a very active theater life. Most plays are in Greek and the season runs from September to May.

Classical Theater. The tragedies of Aeschylus, Sophocles and Euripides, and the comedies of Aristophanes are performed during the summer in ancient theaters all over Greece. The most important ancient theater is at Epidauros in the Peloponnese. The Herod Atticus Theater at the foot of the Acropolis presents both classical drama and other events such as opera and concerts.

Shadow Folk Theater. *Karaghiozis* is the famous shadow puppet theater. It was first introduced from Turkey in the 1830's. The plays are performed by one person behind a screen holding the puppets on a stick. The audience watches the shadows on the screen cast by the puppets. The plays are entertaining and amusing, with humor similar to the slapstick of Punch and Judy. The lead character, *Karaghiozis,* is a poor and uneducated hunchback who survives by his cunning. Because it was political, portraying everyday life as a popular spectacle with political, nationalist, and social class overtones, *Karaghiozis* was extremely popular in the early 20th century. It is no longer performed regularly, but it is worth watching out for.

Folk Art

Folk arts in Greece include embroidery, weaving, metalwork, ceramics, silverwork, sculpture, painting, and architecture. These were often done in home workshops, but this is extremely rare today. Though still practiced, they are often not as traditional as in the past. Folk art themes have been inspired by strong local traditions, Byzantine art, and nature.

Embroidery can be seen in houses and churches, and on traditional clothing. Traditionally a young girl and her mother would embroider colorful and intricate designs on bedsheets and pillowcases for the daughter's trousseau.

Weaving was done at home on a loom, again often for a trousseau. Both woven fabrics for clothing and woven carpets like *kilims* or *flokatis* were produced. Materials used were animal fibers such as wool, goat's hair, and silk; and plant fibers including cotton, flax, and hemp.

Silverware is crafted for both ecclesiastical and secular use in small factories. The most famous silver-producing center is still Ioannina in Epirus.

Metalwork, in copper, bronze, iron, or pewter, are crafted to make household objects such as coffee pots and cooking vessels, or for agricultural tools.

Ceramics are both decorative and functional. Various regions have their own easily recognizable styles, the most well known being from Rhodes and Skyros.

Wood carving is seen on furniture or on doors and ceilings in homes, on shepherds' crooks, and on the *iconostasis* in churches. An ornate baroque carving style is popular. It is incised, carved, or painted, and sometimes it is inlaid with ivory or silver.

Each region has its own folk **architecture**. Mykonos, for example, has cubist whitewashed homes with outside stairways, a balcony, chimney, and lacy dovecotes. The wooden doors, windows, and balcony railings are generally painted blue and there are lace curtains in the windows. The streets, as well as homes, are whitewashed. The 'cave' homes of Santorini, dug out of the cement-like volcanic ash, are another example of folk or vernacular architecture.

Music

Greece has a rich and varied musical history. Greeks are fond of their music, and it still thrives today. Song lyrics dramatically describe the human condition in all its aspects: love, sorrow, war, patriotism, and politics.

Some typical instruments are:

Bouzouki – a long-necked
  mandolin-like instrument.
Baglama – a miniature bouzouki used
  in Rembétika.
Clarinet (*klárino*) – gypsy music is often
  accompanied by the clarinet.
Lute (*laoúto*) – like the Turkish/Arab oud.
Lyra (*líra*) – a 3-stringed fiddle played on the
  thigh rather than shoulder.
Guitar (*kithara*), **Violin** (*vióli*),
Lap drum (*toumberíeki*), **Tambourine** (*défi*),
Goat-skin bag pipe (*tsamboúna*),
Hammer dulcimer (*sandoúri*),
and **Flute** (*fláouto*)

Some musical genres in Greece are:

Byzantine chants and hymns are monophonic songs sung in church. There are different songs for different occasions.

Dhimotiká (folk ballads) were developed during the Turkish occupation and are strongly related to Greek identity. They are songs of freedom, death, suffering, love, heroism, persecution and pain. They are sung at weddings and other festive occasions. *Dhimotiká* are accompanied by the guitar, lute, violin, lap drum, and tambourine. Each region of Greece has its own *dhimotiká* songs.

Kléftic ballads were composed and sung during the Turkish occupation among the *kléfts* (bandits) about the struggle for freedom and heroic deeds.

Kantádhes (Serenades) originated on the Ionian Islands, which didn't experience Turkish occupation. They are an Italian-influenced type of music, usually about love, and accompanied by the guitar and mandolin.

Mirolóyia are death laments. Mourning, especially by women, is expressed outwardly. Death laments are sung by elderly women in the villages who improvise lyrics honoring the dead. The Mani and Mykonos are famous for their *mirolóyia*.

Rembétika are a form of urban blues of a dispossessed sub-culture. It flourished among the refugees from Smyrna (Izmir) on Asia Minor in the 1920's. Themes are love, hashish, prisoners, the underclass, and sorrow. It expresses the philosophy of the *rembétes*, those who live on the margins of society. *Rembétika* songs are punctuated with the Turkish lyrics *amán, amán* (alas, alas). The two most common instruments are the *bouzouki* and *baglama*. In its early years it was looked down upon in Greece, but it's revered nowadays, and can be heard in special *rembétika* clubs. Markos Vamvakaris and Vassilis Tsitsanis are two of the most famous composers and singers of this genre.

Laiká (popular folk songs) emerged from the *Rembétika* tradition in the 1950's. They are songs of the human condition with themes of love, anguish and the hardships of the working class. Some well-known *laiká* composers and singers are Stelios Kazantzidis and Akis Panou.

Entekhno is orchestrated music (literally "artistic") using folk instruments and melodies which also came out of the *Rembétika* tradition in the 1950's. Mikis Theodorakis and Manos Hatzidakis are the two best known composers of this genre.

73

The Greek Archives (FM Records, Greece) has produced many fine anthologies of old recordings such as dhimotiká and rembétika on CD. Box notes have English translations of the lyrics.

A dance of Epirus   *A dance of the Peloponnese*

Dances

When the *kefi* strikes, many Greeks love to dance. One of the most common dances is the *sirtó*, a line dance with each person holding their neighbor's hand. It moves in a counterclockwise circle with eleven shuffling steps. The leader of the dance holds a handkerchief and performs improvisational twirls and gyrations. The *chasapisérviko* is another line dance that is livelier.

The *zebeíko* is danced solo or with two persons face to face. It is interpretative, with solemn overtones, and may involve slapping the heels and hissing. Friends sometimes kneel at the dancers feet and clap. Traditionally only men danced this dance, but now women also do.

The *chasápiko* and *sirtáki* (Zorba's dance) are similar to each other; two or three dancers facing in the same direction with an arm on each other's shoulders. There are set steps, which the leader signals to the other dancers by naming them or with a touch on the shoulder. The *chasápiko* is a little more serious and the *sirtáki* more lively.

The *tséfte téli* is a lively belly dance danced by both men and women.

The *bállos* is a dance for couples facing each other flirtatiously with lively steps.

Every region of Greece has its own local dances. These can be seen at Dora Stratou Theater in Athens.

The Greek Language

"It's Greek to me." You probably know more Greek than you think you do. For instance, psychology, anthropology, gynecology, and the like, are all Greek words; so are our phobias: claustrophobia, acrophobia, agoraphobia as well as our manias: kleptomania, dipsomania, nymphomania. Other English words that come from Greek are chaos, eulogy, polychrome, pathos, rhetoric, paragraph, perimeter, and the list goes on and on. In fact one third of English words have Greek roots.

About 20% of Greek vocabulary is adopted foreign words. There are French words like *crayon* (lipstick) and *maillot* (bathing suit). There are plenty of English words around, too, like parking, self-service, and OK. You're also bound to hear expressions that are part Greek and English like *"íme polí* down *símera!"* (I'm feeling down today!)

Historical Perspective

Greek, in one form or another, has been spoken for nearly 4,000 years making it the oldest spoken language in Europe. Like all languages Greek has changed over the centuries. The Ancient Greek spoken during Classical times evolved into the language of Alexander the Great, Hellenistic Greek, or *koíne.* The New Testament was originally written in *koíne* Greek. The language spoken today is *Dhimotikí* or Modern (Demotic) Greek. The English expression "the common coin" refers to any language that is widely spoken in some area of the world.

Demotic Greek is spoken everywhere today. But in modern times this hasn't always been the case. It had serious competition from *katharévousa* or "clean" Greek as the official language. *Katharévousa* is a purist form closer to the classical and Hellenistic with a complex grammar, syntax, and diction. This linguistic debate was tied to ideology and politics, with the conservatives advocating the purist form and the more liberal left the demotic. The official language switched back and forth between *katharévousa* and *dhimotikí* several times over the years, depending on who was in power. The last reign of *katharévousa* was during the military dictatorship from 1967-1974. After democracy was restored *dhimotikí* was brought back and is the official language in Greece today.

The implications of having *katharévousa* as the official language were enormous. Being the language of schools, government, the law, newspapers, and prestigious professions, it was an elitist language which meant that the vast majority of the population, many of whom were uneducated, could not have access to these services. Many writers such as Kazantzakis and Ritsos wrote in *dhimotikí*.

In Greek, Greece is called *Ellás* (Hellas) or *Elládha*. Greeks are *Éllinas* (male) or *Ellinídha* (female). The Greek language is *Elliniká*.

Pronunciation Guide

The Greek alphabet may seem daunting at first, but it's quite easy to master. Greek is a phonetic language, so once you get the pronunciation down, it comes easier. To be understood, it is important to take care to put the stress on the right syllable. The stressed syllable is shown by the accent mark when writing in the lower case. There are twenty four letters with seven vowels, seventeen consonants, and ten diphthongs.

Greek	Transliteration	Pronunciation	Name
A α	a	'a' as in f<u>a</u>ther	alfa
B β	v	'v' as in <u>v</u>et	vita
Γ γ	g/y	guttural 'g' before consonants or *a, o* or *ou* 'y' as in <u>y</u>ou before an *e* or *i*	gamma
Δ δ	dh	hard 'th' as in <u>the</u>	delta
E ε	e	'e' as in b<u>e</u>t	epsilon
Z ζ	z	'z' as in <u>z</u>oo	zita
H η	i	'ee' as in m<u>ee</u>t	ita
Θ ϑ	th	soft 'th' as in **think**	thita
I ι	i	'ee' as in m<u>ee</u>t	yiota
K κ	k	'k' as in <u>k</u>ing	kapa
Λ λ	l	'l' as in <u>l</u>ove	lamdha
M μ	m	'm' as in <u>m</u>ay	mi
N ν	n	'n' as in <u>n</u>o	ni

Ξ ξ	ks	**'ks'** as in _extra_	_ksi_
O o	o	**'o'** as in _old_	_omikron_
Π π	π	**'p'** as in _pay_	_pi_
P ρ	r	rolled **'r'** sound	_ro_
Σ σ, ς	s	**'s'** as in _sun_	_sigma_
T τ	t	**'t'** as in _time_	_taf_
Y υ	i	**'ee'** as in _meet_	_ipsilon_
Φ φ	f	**'f'** as in _fun_	_fi_
X χ	ch	harsh, throaty **'ch'** (like _loch_)	_chi_
Ψ ψ	ps	**'ps'** as in _lips_	_psi_
Ω ω	o	**'o'** as in _old_	_omega_

Diphthongs

AI	e	**'e'** as in _bet_
AY	av/af	**'av'** or **'af'** depending on the following consonant
EI	i	**'ee'** as in _meet_
OI	i	**'ee'** as in _meet_
EY	ev/ef	**'ev'** or **'ef'** depending on following consonant
OY	ou	**'ou'** as in _ouzo_
ΓΓ	ng	**'ng'** as in _angle_
ΓΚ	g/ng	hard **'g'** at beginning of word; **'ng'** in the middle
ΜΠ	b	**'b'** as in _bar_
NT	d/nd	**'d'** at beginning of word; **'nd'** in the middle

Gamma, ro, and _chi_ (Γ, Π and X) present the main pronunciation difficulties for English speakers. Note that there are five long _e_'s (i), which can cause complications in spelling.

There are no 'ch' or 'sh' sounds in Greek, so "cheeseburger" is _tsisburger,_ "chips" are _tsips,_ and the English name "Sharon" is _Saron._

77

Some Basic Grammar

There is no rigid sentence word order in Greek. The subject, verb, and object can occupy almost any position in the sentence; the meaning doesn't vary much, though different word orders shift the emphasis slightly.

Definite Articles are divided into three genders: masculine, feminine, and neuter. There are three main cases: nominative (subject), possessive, and accusative (object), and there are singular and plural forms for all three cases. An article must agree with the noun in gender, case, and number. There is also a vocative case, which is nearly always the same as the nominative and used when somebody is being addressed.

Singular	Masculine	Feminine	Neuter
Nominative	o	i	to
Possessive	tou	tis	tou
Accusative	ton	tin	to

Plural	Masculine	Feminine	Neuter
Nominative	i	i	ta
Possessive	ton	ton	ton
Accusative	tous	tis	ta

Nouns and **Adjectives** also have three genders. There is not necessarily any rhyme or reason for what gender something takes; for example, "beer" is feminine and "wine" is neuter. The gender should be memorized when the noun is learned. All adjectives, like articles, have to agree with the noun in gender, case, and number. For example, the nominative case for each gender is:

	Singular	Plural	
Masculine	o kalós patéras	i kalí patéres	the good father(s)
Feminine	i kalí mitéra	i kalés mitéres	the good mother(s)
Neuter	to kaló pedhí	ta kalá pedhiá	the good child(ren)

Note that in these examples the article is used and that the adjective comes before the noun.

Personal Pronouns.

In Greek, subject pronouns don't have to be used because the subject is indicated by the inflected verb. However, they are used for emphasis, and you can make yourself more easily understod by using them until you have mastered the verb conjugations.

Singular	Subject Pronouns		Direct Object	Indirect Object
I	egó	me	me	mou
you	esí	you	se	sou
he	aftós	him	ton	tou
she	aftí	her	tin	tis
it	aftó	it	to	tou
Plural				
we	emís	us	mas	mas
you	esís	you	sas	sas
they (M)	aftí	them	tous	tous
they (F)	aftés	them	tis	tous
they (N)	aftá	them	ta	tous

The direct and indirect objects are always placed before the verb.
Direct object. He saw *us*: *Mas ídhe*
Indirect object. He gave *her* the pen: *Tis éthose to stílo*

Possessive Adjectives

are the same as the indirect objects above. They're placed after the noun, and the article is retained:

	Article	Noun	Possessive adjective
My house:	to	spíti	mou

Verbs

are governed by numerous rules and exceptions. Each verb has a stem inflected according to person, number, tense, aspect, mood, and voice. There are eight tenses; there are three moods (indicative, subjunctive, and imperative); and there are two voices (active and passive).

Active verbs fall into three groups:

> *First Group* ends in ω [(o) in the first person singular] and has the stress in the middle of the verb.

The second group has two variations:

Second Group (A) ends in αω (áo), and has the stress on the **a**
in the first person singular.
Second Group (B) ends in ω (ó) with the stress on the last syllable.

Third Group ends in –ομαι (-ome). This is the same ending as
the passive voice, although it is not necessarily passive
in meaning.

Present Tense. The present simple and present progressive tenses are
the same in Greek. Regular verbs are conjugated as follows:

First Group – present. I play, I am playing (pézo)

	Singular	Plural
1st person	pézo	pézoume
2nd person	pézis	pézete
3rd person	pézi	pézoun

Second Group (A) – present. I walk, I am walking (perpató)

	Singular	Plural
1st person	perpató	parpatáme
2nd person	perpatás	perpatáte
3rd person	perpatá	perpatoún

Second Group (B) – present. I drive, I am driving (odhigó)

	Singular	Plural
1st person	odhigó	odhigoúme
2nd person	odhigís	odhigíte
3rd person	odhigí	odhigoún

Third Group – present. I think, I am thinking (sképtome)

	Singular	Plural
1st person	sképtome	skeptómaste
2nd person	sképtese	sképteste
3rd person	sképtete	sképtonde

While simple present and present progressive are the same in Greek, there is a distinction made between the simple and progressive forms in the past and future tenses.

The verb **to be** has forms similar to those of the third group of verbs.

	Singular	Plural
1st person	*íme*	*ímaste*
2nd person	*íse*	*íste*
3rd person	*íne*	*íne*

Past Tense. The past tense has countless rules and exceptions to its formation. The past progressive is the easiest to try to master. For regular verbs, the conjugation in the past progressive, is as follows:

First Group – past. I was playing (*épeza*)

	Singular	Plural
1st person	*épeza*	*pézame*
2nd person	*épezes*	*pézate*
3rd person	*épeze*	*épezan*

Second Group (A&B) – past. I was walking (*perpatoúsa*)

	Singular	Plural
1st person	*perpatoúsa*	*perpatoúsame*
2nd person	*perpatoúses*	*perpatoúsate*
3rd person	*perpatoúse*	*perpaoúsan*

Note that the endings are the same as in the first group, except 'oús' is added to the stem before the ending.

Third Group – past. I was thinking (*skeptómoun*)

	Singular	Plural
1st person	*skeptómoun*	*skeptómaste*
2nd person	*skeptósoun*	*skeptósaste*
3rd person	*skeptótan*	*sképtondan*

Future Tense. The future progressive is easier than the simple and can be formed by simply adding 'tha' (θα) before the present form of the verb.

Irregular Verbs. There are numerous irregular verbs which, as in English, have to be memorized. Some of the more common are as follows:

	Present	Simple Past	Future
to have	écho	ícha	tha écho
to see	vlépo	ídha	tha dhó
to eat	trógo	éfaga	tha fáo
to drink	píno	ípia	tha pió
to go	paó	píga	tha páo
to give	dhíno	édhosa	tha dhóso
to take	pérno	píra	tha páro
to put	vázo	évala	tha válo
to write	gráfo	égrapsa	tha grápso
to want	thélo	íthela	tha thélo
to do	káno	ékana	tha káno
to know	kséro	íksera	tha kséro
to say	léo	ípa	tha pó
to stay	méno	émina	tha míno
to bring	férno	éfera	tha féro
to leave	févgo	éfiga	tha fígo

The **affirmative** and **interrogative** forms are the same. In speech the **interrogative** has a rising intonation at the end of the sentence. In written Greek it is followed by a Greek question mark, which is the English semicolon (;). The **negative** is formed by adding 'then' (δεν) before the verb.

Question Words:

Where?	poú;	How?	pós;
When?	póte;	What?	tí;
Who? (M)	piós;	Who? (F)	piá;
Why?	yatí;		

Can and Must

can	boró	must, have to	prépi
could	boroúsa	should	éprepe

"Can" is conjugated; "must" isn't. They're followed by **'na'**; then the verb.
Can you go? Borís na pás; You must go. Prépi na pás.

82

Some Useful Conjunctions and Adverbs

if	*án*	because	*epíthi/yatí*	when	*ótan*
then	*tóte*	but	*alá*	and	*ké*
or	*i*	in order to	*yía ná*	before	*prín*
that	*pós/óti*	a lot	*polí*	now	*tóra*
soon	*se lígo*	together	*mazí*	far	*makriá*
near	*kondá*				

Prepositions

se   to, at, in, on
> Note: *"se"* combines with the definite article;
> for example: *s'tin Elladha*   In Greece

apó	from, of	*yía*	for, about
mé	with, by, on	*prós*	toward
chorís	without	*méchri*	until
sán	like	*ánti*	instead of
pará	of, before, to	*mazí*	with

Numbers

1	*éna, mía*	11	*éndheka*	60	*eksínda*
2	*dhío*	12	*dhódheka*	70	*evdhomínda*
3	*tría*	13	*dhekatría*	80	*ogdhónda*
4	*tésera*	14	*dhekatésera*	90	*enenínda*
5	*pénde*	etc.	through 19	100	*ekató*
6	*éksi*	20	*íkosi*	150	*ekatopenínda*
7	*eptá*	21	*íkosi éna*	200	*dhiakóssia*
8	*októ*	30	*triánda*	300	*triakóssia*
9	*ennéa*	40	*saránda*	400	*tetrakóssia*
10	*dhéka*	50	*penínda*	1000	*chília*

first *próto*   second *dhéftero*   third *tríto*

Time Words

Sunday	*Kiriakí*	January	*Ianouários*
Monday	*Dheftéra*	February	*Fevrouários*
Tuesday	*Tríti*	March	*Mártios*
Wednesday	*Tetárti*	April	*Aprílios*
Thursday	*Pémpti*	May	*Máios*
Friday	*Paraskeví*	June	*Ioúnios*
Saturday	*Sávato*	July	*Ioúlios*
hour	*óra*	August	*Avgoústos*
day	*méra*	September	*Septémvrios*
week	*evdhomádha*	October	*Októvrios*
month	*mínas*	November	*Noémvrios*
year	*chrónos*	December	*Dhekémvrios*
today	*símera*	tomorrow	*ávrio*
yesterday	*chthés*	this year	*fétos*
last year	*pérsi*	next year	*tou chrónou*

Other Useful Words

yes	né, málista	no	óchi
okay	endáksi	certainly	vevéos, sígoura
now	tóra	later	argótera
open	aniktó	closed	klistó
here	edhó	there	ekí
this one	aftó	that one	ekíno
more	perisótero	less	ligótero
a little	lígo	a lot	polí
good	kaló	bad	kakó
big	megálo	small	mikró
hot	zestó	cold	krío
quickly	grígora	slowly	sigá
near	kondá	far	makriá
cheap	ftinó	expensive	akrivó
left	aristerá	right	dheksiá

84

Some Useful Expressions and Vocabulary

Note: Expressions that are slashed (/) indicate informal and formal or plural address.

Greetings and Goodbyes

Good day	*kalí méra/sas*	Good evening	*kalí spéra/sas*
Good night	*kalí níchta/sas*	Hello	*yia sou/sas or chérete*
Goodbye	*yia sou/sas or adío*	How are you?	*Ti kánis/kánete;*

Essential Expressions

excuse me	*signómi*	please	*parakaló*
thank you	*evcharistó*	(very much)	*pára polí*
it's nothing	*típota*	it doesn't matter	*dhén pirázi*
bon voyage	*kaló taksídhi*	welcome	*kalós ílthate*
good luck	*kalí tíchi*	same to you	*epísis*
come on	*éla*	so-so	*étsi k'étsi*

Useful Expressions

How are you? *Ti kánis/kánete;* Fine. *Kalá* And you? *Ke esí/esís;*
Pleased to meet you. *Chárika (polí)* Me, too. *Ke egó*
What's your name? *Pos se/sas léne;* My name is... *Me léne...*
Where are you from? *Apó pou ísa/ísete;* I'm from.... *Ime apó.....*
What time is it? *Ti óra íne;* I don't know. *Dhén kséro*
How much does it cost? *Póso káni;* Do you understand? *Katalevénete;*
I don't understand. *Dhén katalavéno*
Do you speak English? *Milás/miláte angliká;*
We'll talk later. *Tha ta poúme* Let's go. *Páme*
See you tomorrow. *Tha se tho ávrio.*

Getting Around

hotel	*ksenodhochío*	bed	*kreváti*
room	*dhomátio*	toilet	*toualéta*
women's	*yinekón*	men's	*andrón*
store	*magazí*	kiosk	*períptero*
post office	*tachidhromío*	stamp	*grammatósima*
letter	*grámma*	envelope	*fákelos*
post card	*kárta*	telephone	*tiléfono*
bank	*trápeza*	bakery	*foúrnos*
market	*agorá*	pharmacy	*farmakío*
doctor	*yatrós*	hospital	*nosokomío*

police *astinomía*	station *stathmós*
bus *leoforío*	bus stop *stási*
airplane *aeropláno*	airport *aerodhrómio*
taxi *taksí*	train *tréno*
boat *karávi*	harbor *limáni*
car *aftokínito*	bicycle *podhílato*
ticket *isitírio*	road *dhrómos*
beach *paralía*	church *eklisía*
ancient ruins *archéa*	center *kéntro*
square *platía*	sea *thálassa*
village *chorió*	city *pólis*
Greek fishing boat, also used for short trips *kaíki*	

Some Typical Greek Expressions

Many of these expressions have a corresponding gesture; they are easy to learn by watching.

Ách!	Oh! Ah!
Chrónia pollá	"Many years." Said at name-days, birthdays, etc.
Dhén pirázi	"It doesn't matter" or "No Problem"
Dhiladhí	"For example," "I mean to say..."
Dhóxa to theó	"Glory to God." Said when asked how you are, means essentially "Fine, thanks be to God."
Égine	"It happened." Said when you ask someone to do something for you, meaning it will be attended to right away.
Égine hamós	"All hell broke loose."
Éla!	"Come!", but can also mean "Say something!" or "No way!"
Éla panayía mou!	"Come Virgin Mother and help me!" (Make the sign of the cross) To show surprise or shock.
Filákia	"Kisses." said when ending a conversation, on the phone or in person with a good friend.
Kaiménos/i	"poor dear" said affectionately.
Kakómiros/I	"ill-fated one" meant with compassion.
Kaló dhrómo	"Good road." said when a friend is on their way home or somewhere.

Kaló ríziko	"Good fate" on a new purchase (Congratulations.)
Kríma	"What a pity."
Ksero ego;	"How should I know?"
Lipón	"well", "so", "now", "then"
Makári	"I hope so."
Malákas	"Jerk off." used in many different instances. Not advisable for foreigners to say (especially women).
Na!	Said with the right arm extended, palm forward and five fingers extended (*moútza*). The most disparaging gesture in Greece. Not recommended.
Náse kalá	"Be well" said at the response to a favor
No Problem!	Said in English in response to foreigners who are concerned about things they probably have a good reason to be concerned about.
Ópa!	"Look out!"or in a taverna when the *kefi* is high "Great!"
Oríste;	"May I help you?"
Panayía mazí sou	"May the Virgin Mother be with you." Said if you inadvertently cast the evil eye by complimenting someone, or said as a leavetaking.
Pedhía	"guys"
Perástika	"Get well soon."
Po-po-po!	Any number of things: "Oh la la." "Check that out." "You wouldn't believe it."
Sigá-sigá	"Take it easy." or "Slow down."
Sto kalo	"To the good." a leave taking.
Télos pánton	Said to change from one topic to the next.
Ti yínete;	"What's happening?"
Ti na kanoúme;	"What can we do?" (Our struggles are many.)
Ti néa;	"What's new?"

Greek courses can be taken on-line, or in classes at the Hellenic-American Union, 22 Massalias St. in Athens (www.hau.gr, (210) 368-0000)

Some Useful Websites

www.gogreece.com An excellent site for information on all aspects of Greece including history, education, religion, business and travel.

www.gtp.gr Up-to-date travel information including ferry schedules.

www.usembassy.gr Information on all aspects of visa requirements for Americans in Greece, including extensions on tourist visas, residence permits, etc. Also information on getting married in Greece for U.S. citizens.

www.athensnews.gr The Athens News on-line.

www.ekthimerini.com The Greek section of the International Herald Tribune on-line.

www.HAU.gr Greek lessons in classroom or on-line.

...and Phone Numbers

Embassies: U.S.A.   (210) 721-2951-9

    Canada   (210) 727-3400

    U.K.   210) 727-2600

    Australia   (210) 645-0404

Tourist Police

    (Boat schedule, hotels, etc. in English)   171

Bus Schedule in Athens   185

Directory Assistance   131

Police Emergency Service   100

Police Call Center (Non emergency)   133

Ambulance   166

Hospitals and Pharmacies on Duty (Athens area)   1434

Telephone Information   131

International Call Information (English)   169

Taxis (one reliable company of many)   1203

Ombudsman (Assistance with bureaucratic issues)   (210) 363-9640

Some Books about Greece

Ancient History

Bowra, Maurice. *The Greek Experience.* (Cardinal) Ancient Greek history and art.

Burn, A.R. *The Pelican History of Greece.* (Penguin) General scholarly introduction to Ancient Greece.

Finley, M.I. *The Ancient Greeks.* (Penguin) General introduction to Ancient Greece.

Pollitt, J.J. *Art and Experience in Classical Greece.* (Cambridge University Press) Wonderful and clear explanation of the evolution of art forms from the Archaic to the Hellenistic Period.

Starr, Chester G. *The Ancient Greeks.* (Oxford University Press) The rise and fall of ancient Greece, as well as developments and changes in art and philosophy. Illustrated.

Modern Greek History

Boatswain, Timothy and Nicolson, Colin. *A Traveller's History of Greece.* (Interlink Books) A concise overview of Greek history from Prehistoric times to the present for travelers to Greece interested in history.

Clogg, Richard. *A Concise History of Greece.* (Cambridge University Press). From the fall of Byzantium through 1991. Concise and well-written.

Fourtouni, Eleni. *Greek Women in Resistance.* (Thelphini Press) Journals and oral history of women warriors during World War II and the Civil War.

Koliopoulos, John S. and Veremis, Thanos M. *Greece: The Modern Sequel From 1831 to the Present.* (Hurst & Co.) A thematic view of Modern Greek history including politics, ideology, and foreign policy.

Michas, Takis. *Unholy Alliance.* (Texas A & M University Press) A critical examination of why the Greeks supported Milosevic and the Serbs during the recent conflicts in the former Yugoslavia.

Pettifer, James. *The Greeks: The Land and People Since the War.* (Penguin) An excellent historical and social account of Greece since World War II.

Woodhouse, C.M. *Modern Greece: A Short History* (Faber & Faber) Woodhouse fought in the Greek resistance during WWII. A right-wing perspective.

Ethnology

Campbell, John K. *Honor, Family and Patronage.* (Oxford University Press) Study of the honor and shame value system among the Sarakatsani shepherds in Northern Greece during the 1950's.

Dubisch, J. (ed.) *Gender and Power in Rural Greece.* (Princeton University Press) Anthology of works on women's issues by various ethnographers.

Friedl, Ernestine. *Vasilika: A Village in Modern Greece.* (Holt, Rinehart and Winston) Seminal anthropological work conducted in Greece in the late 1950's.

Herzfeld, Michael. *The Poetics of Manhood: Contest and Identity in a Cretan Mountain Village.* (Princeton University Press) The author's fieldwork in a Cretan village.

Holst, Gail. *Road to Rembétika: Songs of Love, Sorrow, and Hashish.* (Denise Harvey & Co.) Social history and music of the Greek subculture that produced *rembétika*, the Greek blues.

Loizos, Peter and Evthymios Papataxiarchis (eds.) *Contested Identities: Gender and Kinship in Modern Greece* (Princeton University Press) Various ethnographers' work revolving around gender issues. Excellent anthology.

Religion

Constantinidou-Partheniadou, Sofia. *A Travelogue in Greece and Folklore Calendar.* (Athine). A comprehensive overview of Greek religious holidays and saint's days. May be difficult to find.

Ware, Timothy, *The Orthodox Church.* (1993) An overview of the history and theology of Orthodoxy.

Greek Literature in Translation

Dalven, Rae. *The Complete Poems of Cavafy.* (Harcourt, Brace, Jovanovich) Excellent translation of the complete works of Cavafy, in chronological order.

Friar, Kimon. *Modern Greek Poetry.* (Simon and Schuster) An anthology of Modern Greek poetry including works of two Nobel laureates, Odysseus Elytis and George Seferis.

Kazantzakis, Nikos. *Zorba.* Quintessentially Greek with kefi and soul. *Freedom or Death.* The story of Captain Michalis and the liberation of Crete.

Keeley, Edmund. *Ritsos in Parentheses.* (Princeton University Press) Poetry of Yannis Ritsos. Facing page in Greek and English.

Kostis, Nicholas (Translator), *Modern Greek Short Stories.* (Odysseus Publications) Representative anthology of Greek short stories in the 19th and 20th centuries.

Modern Greek Poetry. (Efstathiadis Group) Anthology featuring George Seferis and Odysseus Elytis.

Papadiamantis, Alexandros. *Tales from a Greek Island.* (Johns Hopkins University Press) Short stories of life on a Greek island at the end of the 19th century.

Sotiriou, Dido. *Farewell Anatolia.* (Kedros Publishers). A story depicting the end of Greek life in Asia Minor.

Stories about Greece

DeBernieres, Louis. *Captain Corelli's Mandolin.* (Vintage Books) A love story between an Italian and a Greek woman on the island of Cefallonia during World War II.

Durrell, Gerald. *My Family and Other Animals.* (Penguin) Funny and fabulous account of a young boy naturalist living in Corfu in the 1930's

Durrell, Lawrence. *Prospero's Cell.* (Marlowe & Co.) An anecdotal and romantic portrayal of Corfu in the 1930's.
Bitter Lemons. (Marlowe & Co.) Durrell's description of living as an English teacher in Northern Cyprus in the 1940's.

Falacci, Oriana. *A Man.* (Schuster) An account of the relationship between the author and the man who attempted to assassinate Colonel Papadopoulos, the leader of the junta.

Fowles, John. *The Magus.* (Dell) Magic and mystery on a Greek island in the 1950's. (fiction)

Gage, Nicholas. *Eleni.* (Ballentine) The author's account of his family in northern Greece during the Civil War.

Keeley, Edmund. *Inventing Paradise: The Greek Journey. 1937-1947.* (Northwestern University Press) A portrayal of Henry Miller, Lawrence Durrell, George Seferis, and other writers in Greece before World War II.

Travel Writing

Gage, Nicholas. *Hellas: A Portrait of Greece.* (Efstathiadis Group) Out of print in the U.S. but widely available in Greece.

Fermer, Patrick Leigh. *Roumeli.* (Penguin) and *Mani.* (Penguin) Informative and easy to read travel stories from the 50's by a philhellene who fought in the Cretan resistance during World War II.

Miller, Henry. *The Colossus of Maroussi.* (New Directions) A descriptive look into the soul of Greece in 1939.

A Cookbook

Kochilas, Diane. *The Glorious Foods of Greece.* (William Morrow). Recipes from all over the country with historical and traditional background.

Movies in English about Greece

Captain Corelli's Mandolin (2001) Dir: John Madden with Nicholas Cage, Penelope Cruz. Based on the book by Louis deBerniers about the Italian occupation of Kefalonia during WWII.

Eleni (1985) Dir: Peter Yates with Kate Nelligan, John Hurt, and Linda Hunt. Based on the book by Nicholas Gage. A personal account of the Civil War in Greece.

Guns of Navarone (1961) Dir: J. Lee Thompson with Gregory Peck, David Niven, Anthony Quinn, and Irene Papas. World War II adventure.

My Big Fat Greek Wedding (2001) Dir: Joel Zwick with Nia Vardalos and John Corbett. Hilarious account of a Greek American who falls in love with a vegetarian WASP.

Never on Sunday (1960) Dir: Jules Dassin with Melina Mecouri and Jules Dassin. An American amateur philosopher tries to reform a Greek prostitute in Piraeus, who he thinks is symbolic of why Greece is no longer great.

Pascali's Island (1988) Dir: John Deardon with Ben Kinglsey, Helen Mirren, and Charles Dance. Based on the novel by Barry Unsworth about a failed Turkish bureaucrat and the end of the Turkish occupation on a Greek island.

Shirley Valentine (1989) Dir: Lewis Gilbert with Pauline Collins and Tom Conti. A middle-aged Liverpool housewife finds romance on a Greek island.

The Tempest (1982) Dir: Paul Mazursky with John Cassavetes, Gena Rowland, and Susan Sarandon. Modern day version of Shakespeare's play set on a Greek island.

Z (1969) Dir: Costa Gavras with Yves Montand, Irene Papas. Based on the novel by Vassilis Vassilikos about the true account of the assassination of a prominent Greek leftists, Dimitris Lambrakis, that led to the military junta.

Zorba the Greek (1964) Dir: Michael Cacoyannis with Anthony Quinn, Irene Papas, and Alan Bates. Based on the novel by Nikos Kazantzakis about an uptight Englishman who learns about the joys of life from a lusty Greek.